D0920606

# Caught with my Mouth Open

## WINNIE CHRISTENSEN

Harold Shaw Publishers, Wheaton, Illinois

*Library of Congress Catalog Card Number 77-86529*
*Copyright © 1969 by Harold Shaw Publishers*
*Wheaton, Illinois 60187*
*First printing, June 1969*
*Second printing, October 1969*
*Third printing, July 1970*
*Fourth printing, June 1971*
*Fifth printing, July 1973*
*Sixth printing, February 1977*

**Printed in United States of America**

# Contents

## Acknowledgements

This book relates the personal experiences of many friends. I am grateful for their willingness to share the blessing of God in their lives with others. They answered the questionnaires I sent them with frankness and sincerity. They trusted me to change their names. And they prayed a lot!

I am also grateful to Linda Sofia, Montene Rosone, Marge Prichard and Jennie De Angelo who kept our family from being buried under unironed clothes and dust; to my mother, Mrs. William Englund, for willing, expert baby-sitting while I wrote; to Sharon Carter for typing the manuscript; to Nena Thornton who shared so vitally in these events and in every page; and to my husband and children for enduring the whole process with good grace and humor.

## Introduction

"I'm perfectly willing to help with a neighborhood Bible study group. I'd be delighted to see such a thing started. I'd even open my home for one. But lead it? Not me. I'm just not the type."

The one who spoke was quiet and retiring, one of a group of women who had gathered to talk about having Bible studies in their neighborhoods. Lillian was shy—not the aggressive type at all. Yet strangely enough she was strongly attracted to the idea of a Bible study for her neighbors. She went home that afternoon challenged and saying she would pray about it, but also saying that she was quite confident the Lord would choose someone else to get the whole thing started. To myself I thought, *Don't say that so loud! Someone might hear you—like God!*

The Lord loves to take our rash or emphatic statements and challenge us through them. (Someone else I know prayed fervently one day on his way to work, *Lord, whatever you're going to be doing today, I want to be in on it.* He got to work and was promptly fired, an event that, though shattering, proved to be one of the best things that ever happened to him.)

A few weeks later one of Lillian's neighbors spent some time visiting with her while Lillian sorted her laundry in the basement. The woman finally said good-bye and turned to leave. Halfway up the stairs she stopped and said, "Lillian, if you ever start a Bible study, I'll come."

It was a bolt out of the blue. They had never even discussed studying the Bible. Lillian said, "I felt as though the Lord had hit me on the head with a hammer. But he got his message across. *I* started a *Bible study*!"

In a very real sense this is the story of this book. *Once I opened my mouth,* the Lord took me at my word. There was no backing out. But he also took over. When it's a venture of faith, done in his name, he never leaves us to flounder alone. It becomes *his* venture. God meant it when he said "Open your mouth wide, and I will fill it."[1] I opened my mouth and God filled it—with his own words!

[1] Ps. 81:10 (RSV).

# 1

## Study Circle

It was a brisk March morning with the sun pouring in through the windows of a suburban living room. There was nothing unusual about the home or the fact that a group of women were sitting there drinking coffee. Coffee-klatsching is the usual thing among neighborly homemakers. What made this group noticeably different was that in addition to holding a coffee cup, each woman was also looking into an open Bible.

Rhoda, young mother of five, was leading a discussion this morning on chapter 10 of the book of Romans.

"How does the Apostle Paul contrast man's idea of righteousness with what God says is the way to become righteous?" she asked.

"Well, man thinks he's good enough for God, or

at least can make himself good enough for God, but God says he can't."

"Here we go again," another woman wryly added. "Paul has been telling us for chapters on end how rotten we are and he's still rubbing it in. I feel like saying, 'Lay off, Paul, I get your point. I'm cowed and beaten.' "

"Yes, he leaves us with little room for self-confidence or self-satisfaction after calling us ignorant, disobedient, selfish, evil, proud, unrighteous, sinners, and a few other such choice epithets."

"But if we're that bad, and the Bible surely says we are," interjected Rhoda, "how can we become good enough to please God?"

A thoughtful pause followed as each woman looked carefully at the verses before her, and then one responded, "According to what it says here, it's faith in Jesus Christ that makes a person right with God."

My eyes glanced around the group. Some were deep in thought. Others seemed to be consciously trying to avoid thinking. Alice was staring off into space. She had been raised on this kind of teaching and had been soured by hearing one thing preached and seeing another thing lived by those who thought they were Christians. She had little love for Christians. Her criterion for judging her own spiritual status seemed to be that she must be right with God because everything was going along so smoothly in her life.

Then there was Jill, quiet, alert, mature in spite of her youth, and drinking in every word. Jane, beside her, was impassive. She was skilled at turning the study off. It was as though she were afraid that any penetration would demand too much of her. In fact, all of us seemed to play this game with varying degrees of proficiency.

Some women chose not to play the game at all. If the personal conflict produced by exposure to the Bible became too great, they just stayed away. Few women were as openly honest as one who attended only a few times and then candidly admitted, "I'm not a joiner. I'm not a goer. I'm not a student. Bible study is real misery and agony for me. I'd sooner scrub the floor. So if I attend a Bible study group it sure as hell better be good!" Fortunately, for the study, most of the women didn't share this viewpoint. They enjoyed a morning away from household chores, and they appreciated adult conversation.

One woman had belonged to a church-sponsored discussion therapy group but found it unsatisfactory. She said, "Everyone aired their problems, but no one had any solutions. Here, at least we get a few solutions from the Bible." Someone else affectionately dubbed our study "the Wednesday group therapy."

Myrtle openly carried her bag of worries and fears. If something bothered her, and it usually did, we all knew about it. But she endeared herself to all the women with her frank observations about everything. She often said, "This is the only place I can go, be completely myself, and not worry about being accepted."

Pat was an enthusiast. She had come in contact with Jesus Christ only recently, and she constantly bubbled with the excitement of knowing him. I couldn't help hoping that her new faith would always be as fresh and vibrant as it was this day.

I looked at the two widows in our group. They were so young to be left responsible for growing families. One had learned of her widowhood when a state trooper had knocked on her door in the middle of the night. He told her that her husband had been killed in an automobile accident. She was left with three preschool children. The other woman watched her husband die a slow death over a period of ten years from an unusual blood disease. She was left with two teen-agers. Which was in the most difficult position? Who can tell? But they came to the Bible study out of a sense of their personal need.

It was a special thrill to see Irene back at the study today with her newborn son. According to medical authorities she shouldn't have been there at all. The doctor had warned her that with her rare form of kidney disease she would never survive another pregnancy.

When her first child had been stillborn, the severity of her long-standing kidney ailment was discovered. It was then the doctor warned that another pregnancy would not only take the baby's life but hers as well. She and her husband adopted two children. Then one day she was faced with the reality of impending death in a matter of months, for she found she was again pregnant. She had had "scares" before which had left her distraught and in tears. This time it wasn't a false alarm. It was real, and she couldn't understand why she felt so calm about it. She recalled thinking, *If I die, this is God's plan for me. He will provide a mother for my children. Now, if I have only a few months to live, what can I do to make my life worthwhile?*

It was then that she decided to involve herself with the Bible study, and to make contacts with her neighbors to tell them about Christ. One of the friends she brought later came to know Christ.

All through her pregnancy her sense of tranquillity prevailed. Irene admitted, "I felt sedated, although I wasn't." Her perpetual serenity in the long months of waiting made quite an impact on the group.

Now here she sat among us again. She and the baby were both in good heath, and the doctor had no explanation for it. Some of the women in the group would say, "Of course!—we prayed!" They *expected* miracles.

Helen was another quiet one, but when she spoke she revealed a calm inner depth and knowledge. She was so stable it was hard to picture her coming from a childhood home shattered by alcoholism and divorce. She was partially reared by five bachelor uncles—hardly a normal home atmosphere. But the home she had now established was vastly different, it was cohesive and secure. Christ had worked a miracle in her life too.

Edith's greatest burden was the care of an aged, senile mother. Without complaint she went every day to the nursing home to feed her mother who no longer recognized her. In the Bible study she found strength and comfort for the daily tedium.

Nena, our weekly hostess, was a joyful person. She loved the women. She loved the Bible study, and it showed. The Bible study had transformed her whole pattern of life. Her radiance didn't reveal that she had had to get three children off to school, another child to the nursery, her house in order, and a 30-cup pot of coffee made, all before 9:30 A.M. Her welcome was always genuine and cheerful when the first guest arrived. God had worked a miracle in her too!

Peggy appeared preoccupied. She fought a perpetual battle with self-pity and bottled-up resentments. The chip on her shoulder was heavy today.

My thoughts were interrupted by Rhoda's next question. The discussion went on, spirited sometimes, then quieter and thoughtful. But God's words in the Bible were being applied to each one there. Of course, it hadn't always been like this. In three years we had come a long way.

# 2

## I
## Open
## My
## Mouth

Three years earlier on an October morning our Bible study had started. Before then, I had heard a great deal about the effectiveness of neighborhood Bible studies among women, especially in the Eastern states. It had sounded interesting, and fascinating. But it also seemed scary to me. The fact that I had grown up as a missionary's child with all the advantages of thorough teaching in the Scriptures from my earliest childhood was no comfort. For me the world at large remained a faceless sea of souls in need. But to face people as individuals? Help! What if they asked me something I didn't know? That would make me look stupid, and the thought made me curl up inside.

Yet I kept running into people like Marie Little who had done so much in such studies. This perpetually goaded my conscience as my concern deepened. Of course, it wasn't as though I had avoided all contacts with the outside world. There had been women's groups, Sunday school and children's club. But in these there was a certain sense of security. It was easy to face the world from within the confines of the local church, much as an infant in his crib enjoys life in circumscribed security. This is probably why such a large segment of the evangelical church has made so little impact in the world. We'd rather remain snug, protected and undeveloped.

Some have called it the sin of self-containment—contentment with the status quo. We keep busy with so many church activities and useful projects that we don't have time to make friends with the person next door. A woman, very active in Christian women's organizations, told me recently that she had lived on one street for six years and had never gotten acquainted with a single neighbor. She was just too busy. Unfortunately, this is more the norm than the exception. It may be busyness, or fear, or false ideas about "separation," or prejudice that keeps us from growing and leaving our secure Christian cradle.

For Jesus' disciples, traveling through Samaria one hot, weary day with their Master, the lack of involvement with other people was a combination of racial prejudice and a blinding preoccupation with their physical fatigue and hunger.

That day Jesus met a woman at a well outside of town. He was tired. She was confused. Her life was all mixed up. Jesus faced her with her long string of failures. Then he showed her how to overcome this waste of life, how to start over again. Not just to turn over a clean page, but to start a whole new existence that would stretch into eternity. She had met for the first time in her life one who could condemn but in the same breath offer forgiveness.

How could she keep such news to herself? She hurried to share it with the very townspeople who doubtless had criticized and gossiped about her. But they were just as confused as she was, perhaps only having hid their vices a little more thoroughly, and a long trail of local citizens followed the woman back to meet this amazing Jesus.

The disciples had returned from town earlier, but no one followed *them* back to meet Jesus. They had come back the same self-contained, disgruntled bunch they had been when they left. Was it because they had nothing to share? Or did they decide the town didn't need to know their Master? The need was there all right. This became apparent later as the people eagerly crowded to meet Jesus for themselves.

The problem obviously lay then in the disciples. They were bent on feeding their stomachs. That anyone else might have a greater need didn't enter their heads. They weren't in town to share their

Master, the one who had touched blind eyes with sight, the one who had given strength to lame legs, the one who had even made the dead alive. They had seen all of this. They intimately knew this unique Man. They had heard the things he had spoken with divine authority. Their own lives had been changed. But that seemed unimportant now. Their stomachs were empty. They must have their physical desires met even at the eternal cost of the people with whom they came in contact.

They returned from town with provisions, but otherwise the same. And they met Jesus with criticism in their hearts for lowering himself to talk to a woman—a Samaritan at that. They were surprised—upset that he didn't share their interest in the food they had brought.

This is a lesson that the Lord has emphasized to me over and over again, because it's fatally easy to slip back into this pattern of self-containment. It's also easy to judge other people for their lack of interest in spiritual matters. It's difficult to become personally involved with them.

I prayed for deliverance from such crib-type security. I made myself available to God—a dangerous thing to do. The Lord usually takes us at our word!

**Spotlight
on
Truth**

The Bible study didn't start the next day after I prayed, or the next week. The Lord sometimes moves very quickly. Other times his processes seem painfully slow. But this is really one of the exciting aspects of serving God—the discovery that he is not limited by physical environment, as we are. His times and places are always right. When we try to live in constant contact with him from day to day it takes the worry out of losing time, because God *never* wastes his time, or ours.

In my case the Lord had to do some more groundwork—mostly in me. Through mutual friends, who happened to be missionaries returning to their country of service, I was brought in contact with a young woman who was a new Christian. Their idea was that I would be available to answer some questions she might have and to generally help her grow in her new faith. From that first faltering introduction, we rapidly progressed to a weekly contact in which we hashed out doctrine, scriptural principles, family and home problems. In the end, I learned far more from her than she learned from me. She demanded explanations of my faith in unclicheed terms. She looked for reality in my life. She hated sham. She constantly related what I said to what I did in my home and family situations. It was a discipline. I felt constantly in the spotlight of her scrutiny. However, her motivation was to learn; not to judge. She was never content with the status quo, but devoured truth with insatiable hunger. Her probing honesty brought a fresh vitality to my faith, which was prone to get worn at the edges.

Besides the discipline of making a reasonably tidy house each Tuesday, two years of this yielded us a firm friendship and a mutual realization that no person is quite complete until he has found the missing dimension of his life in a vital relationship with Jesus Christ. Her Christian faith was so exciting and living to her that she wanted everyone to share in it—most of all, her husband. We prayed for him every week. We prayed for her that she wouldn't push too hard—a nagging wife seldom produces a Christian husband. (This is a subject we'll talk about later, for it became a common problem in our group.)

One Tuesday afternoon my friend walked in and her glowing face revealed that our prayer for her husband had been answered. There had been nothing dramatic in the decision. While eating his lunch in solitude at work one day, he had quietly bowed his head and committed his life to Jesus Christ. Then he phoned his wife to say, quite simply, "Well, I did it."

Some excerpts from a recent letter reveal what has happened since then in this friend's life:

"These past years, we've been 'going on,' the Lord and I. The break came when I finally saw my old self—dead and hopeless and not to be trusted. Somehow, without words to explain, I turned myself over to Him and He has been in control ever since. Christ is never out of my range—He's just there all the time. I'm overwhelmed that He's so real and that He's willing to be real to me."

Those weekly sessions taught me more than anything else that knowledge of the Bible alone means very little. It's not how many verses we can recite. It's not how much doctrine we can regurgitate. It's the reality of that knowledge applied to life which will be the greatest evidence that the knowledge is valid to someone else. I'm sure God's not nearly as interested in the quantity of facts we can rattle back to him as in the degree to which all these "facts" were truly lived out in our daily lives. The challenge remains that he will hold us responsible for all we know.

# 4

## Making Friends

Someone has said that the best way to get acquainted with your neighbors is to have either a dog or children. For a while we didn't own the former but happened to fill a house with the latter. Children may be great at breaking the ice, but they're even more expert at breaking windows and digging up flowers. And, on one occasion, our four-year-old boy along with his buddy made a lovely bucket full of mud and painted his friend's new family car *inside* with it—from front to back. This hardly contributed to a feeling of neighborliness, but after the apologies were made and the bills paid, we did manage to come through with some very real friendships with these neighbors.

Fortunately, there were also the positive aspects in making friends of our neighbors—the shared delight of watching our children grow, the joint concern at the times of their illnesses and injuries, the help we gave each other in pushing out-of-gas cars, or borrowing ladders to get in upstairs windows when locked out of our homes, and ultimately the sharing in the deepest sorrow of death.

One morning my next-door neighbor, a young German bride in America only a year, came walking down her driveway with a bewildered look of incredulity on her face.

"What's the matter?" I asked.

"My baby," she said softly. "I found him dead in his crib this morning. He only had a cold. He was all right at midnight, but this morning—" and then her grief overwhelmed her.

We could only love and pray and offer a measure of understanding since we, too, had buried two infants. A number of years later she recalled that among her most cherished memories was that of the help and the prayers and the "silent presence" of her friends and neighbors at that hour of grief. It had an influence on her later attending the Bible study.

There are two basic aspects to making friends. The first is to consciously work at it. The second is to be "available." For the first we actively and consciously seek common ground on which an acquaintance or a friendship can be built, not necessarily within the framework of church-oriented affairs. You invite your neighbor for lunch or dinner, or go to a concert, or browse in an antique store with her. You do your marketing together or pick her up on your way to PTA. Simply find out what interests your neighbor and look for a way to make a positive contact. But after having gone to all that work, don't be disappointed if you are "stood up." Many a luncheon and dinner and even a planned outing have gone begging because the invited friend has "forgotten." Don't write her off your list for having snubbed you. Forgive, forget, pray and try again—always graciously.

Another factor in the conscious effort of making friends should also be considered. What about when we find ourselves associating with people whose standards and morals are quite different from our own? I was at a recent women's conference when this subject came up for discussion. The particular bone of contention in this case was drinking. And one lady declared hotly, "I just wouldn't go to a home where I knew alcoholic beverages would be served because it would ruin my Christian testimony to be seen there! People would think I *approved* of their drinking."

I have had well-meaning Christians ask me in the past (they don't anymore), "Aren't you afraid of what people will think when you allow your friends to smoke in your home?" "What will people say?" "What will people think?" These questions carry more weight for many Christians than what God thinks or how he values individual human lives.

What was Jesus' attitude? He never allowed what people might think of him to get in the way of his helping someone who needed it. To him the value of a human life was far more important than his reputation. His encounter with the woman of Samaria is a classic example of that. He laid his reputation on the line to help this woman who was so desperately searching for answers. What his disciples thought of him made no difference. He hadn't compromised his own standard of life. He didn't condone her sin, but neither did he shun her because of the kind of person she was. He reached out to help.

A woman phoned me recently to tell me she had befriended a neighbor whose reputation in their area was similar to that of the woman of Samaria. This neighbor had a husband. She also had a full-time "boyfriend" who came around when the husband was at work. She even had borne a child out of this illicit relationship. Because of this unsavory situation other neighbors avoided her. But the woman on the phone was a Christian and just couldn't write off her neighbor that easily. So she tried to be her friend. Then she asked, "Winnie, am I compromising my standard by being friendly to this woman?"

I asked, "*Have* you compromised it?"

She quickly replied, "Oh no! In fact, I have told her that I don't approve of what she's doing, but I still love her as a person. And I tell her Christ can help her. She gets mad at me and sometimes won't talk to me for days, but then—she always comes back. I think she needs me for a friend. And I pray for her."

"If you haven't compromised your own standards, then don't worry about what people may think or say. It's far more important to do what God wants and to please him," was my reply.

This is an area in which many of us need to examine our motives carefully. We can't afford to feel superior to anyone because of our social or economic or educational status. This applied to friendships which cross ethnic and color lines as well. Why do we consciously avoid making friends of people who are a different color than we are or who aren't as well educated? Fear of what people will say? Prejudice? Fear of loss of "property value"? What piece of property has a greater value than a human being? The Jews had nothing to do with the Samaritans, but this didn't stop Jesus from making a friend of a Samaritan. Can we do anything less? "A servant is not greater than his master! Nor is the messenger more important than the one who sends him. You know these things— now do them! That is the path of blessing."[1]

[1] John 13:16-17 (*Living Gospels*).

Then, the matter of availability. Often when our conscious efforts fail in making friends, the Lord uses the unexpected to bring people together. Here our lives need to be flexible enough for interruptions by the doorbell or the phone.

One afternoon, one of my neighbors, deeply agitated, dropped in to see me. Her child had been molested at a public park. She desperately needed to share her distressing problem with someone else; she couldn't have cared less how my house looked or how I looked. She needed a sympathic ear right then. If I had turned her away because I was too busy or unprepared for company, she might have been turned off completely for further communication. She also needed to know that her confidence would not be shared with all the neighbors. Though we should open our mouths to share God's good news, keeping our mouths shut about confidences and personal problems is an absolute necessity, hard as it sometimes seems.

Being a friend also means knowing when to withdraw from a prickly situation. One day I was casually chatting with a neighbor woman on the sidewalk. We were joined by another lady and the conversation changed rather quickly from quiet pleasantries to a heated discussion. One woman accused the other's husband of lying in wait for her husband and threatening him with a blackjack! The details of the incident were rather hazy, but there were charges and countercharges, and it took some rather careful stepping on my part to withdraw from the situation without taking sides, and still remain a friend of each. A closed mouth at that point was vital to all concerned. It's an almost irresistible temptation for women to pass on interesting information. Another name for this is gossip! Being a Christian doesn't guarantee that we won't fall prey to this temptation. But in being Christians we have the power to resist it. A great deal more would be accomplished for our Lord if we learned to talk less of such things and pray more.

Making real friends of people—of our neighbors in particular—is of prime importance if we want to communicate Jesus Christ to them.

A Jewish girl who became a Christian in college through the influence of her roomate, made this significant statement: "She was a friend who shared joys and sorrows, a 24-hour-a-day friend. She wasn't false. She wasn't a person who was a friend because she was witnessing, but she was a witness because she was a friend."[2]

Between these two aspects of a relationship there's a world of difference. Christians have been accused of often viewing people merely as souls to be saved, and of being unable to love and accept people just as they are. Admittedly, some people are harder to love than others but, then, maybe

[2] HIS "Study in Witness," (March, 1968), p. 7.

they feel the same way about us! In a day when life has become so impersonal and individuals tend to be reduced to statistics or numbers on an IBM machine, it's all the more imperative that someone relate to them as individuals. No one is better equipped to offer love and personal care for someone else than the person who has experienced the love of Jesus Christ himself. Involvement and availability are a small price to pay when compared with the price Christ paid to make himself available to people, even to those who didn't want him. Not only does Christ give us the power to do what he wants us to do each day, but he offers a "guaranteed wage" as well. This stimulated Paul to encourage us, "And let us not get tired of doing what is right, for after a while we will reap a harvest of blessing if we don't get discouraged and give up."[3]

[3] Gal. 6:9 (*Living Letters*).

# 5

## Two Weeks
## from Wednesday

The Lord started the Bible study. If he had waited until I considered myself ready, we would still be waiting. Our "reasons" for hesitating to plunge into new ventures often become rather flimsy excuses when viewed in honesty before the Lord. In talking to women about starting their own Bible study groups, I have learned that most women are skilled in diversionary tactics. "My house isn't big enough—I could *never* lead—My children are too young—I don't have the time" on and on.

Lack of time is probably the most frequently used excuse. Everybody is busy, especially the homemakers who run taxi service for their children, serve as den mothers, work on committees in their churches, schools or communities, belong to bridge clubs or bowling leagues. There are dozens of different activities that can occupy a house-wife's time in or out of the home.

It boils down then to sorting out priorities, and the safest place to sort them out is on your knees before the Lord. It was here that my concern for a neighborhood Bible study grew and developed. Also a statement attributed to Amy Carmichael, the great missionary to India, came to my mind with disturbing frequency—"There is enough time in each day to do all of God's will for that day." It was obvious that my days were cluttered with nonessentials, because I never seemed to have enough time for *anything* extra!

The next need was a partner to work with. Those who are experienced with Bible studies advise having at least one other person who shares your concern and belief, and who also lives in your general neighborhood. This means that the load of responsibility and leading can be shared. Should one get sick, the other can carry on. Should one be discouraged or bogged down, the other can supply the needed encouragement.

As I prayed about this particular need, the Lord brought to my mind a young family which had started attending our church within the year. They lived within five minutes of us. Somehow Nena seemed to be just the right person for such a venture. All I had to do was phone. Now, the inability to gab has never been recognized as one of my weaknesses. However, to pick up the phone and ask Nena if she were interested in working in a Bible study became a mountainous obstacle. My heart pounded as I dialed her number and, with a great surge of "faith," steeled myself for what I thought would be an almost certain no. I timidly put the question to her and she replied, "Why, I think a neighborhood Bible study is a grand idea. I'd love to be involved. When do we start?" The shock was almost too much, but—it did loosen my tongue and we were on our way.

We arranged a meeting with Marie Little and a few other ladies who were interested in getting some pointers on how to start. I had thought we would attempt our first Bible study a month or two after our planning meeting. Then I heard Nena declare confidently, "Well, I think our first study should be two weeks from Wednesday. I believe in jumping right in. We either sink or swim." I was prepared for drowning!

In that short time we had to get a baby-sitter for the preschoolers, decide where we should meet and, hopefully, obtain neighbors interested enough to come.

There was also that persistent, nagging question "What if someone asks a question I can't answer or presents an argument I can't refute?" This is a common fear. It numbs many women into in-action. We discovered through later experience how simple it is to say, "I don't know the answer to that one, but I'll certainly be glad to see if I can find it for you by next week." No one really expects a Bible study leader to be a walking biblical encyclopedia or textbook on systematic theology. It was also our experience that many times the answer to a question would come from someone else in the group—a double advantage. Not only was the question answered, but someone other than the leader had the chance to help and inform the group.

Nena and I agreed that Marie should lead the first study in the book of Mark to get us launched. Nena decided her home was a good place to meet, and we both got on the phone to call our neighbors. Even though most of them were by now our friends, these calls were not easy to make. I guess, as Christians, we tend to be so much on the defensive in our faith that we just assume no one could possibly be interested in spending one whole morning a week studying the Bible.

We put the question something like this: "We're getting together for coffee and an informal Bible study Wednesday morning. There's no denominational affiliation about it, and you don't have to know anything about the Bible. We're just getting together to see what we can learn. Would you like to join us?"

It was a delightful surprise to get more "yeses" than "noes."

Incidentally, the idea of the Bible study not being related to one particular church or denomination had great appeal for the women who were invited. Furthermore, we never "pushed" any one church. This fact actually lost one woman to a Bible study group. She left after it became apparent that group wasn't going to encourage all its members to become Baptists!

The Lord gave us a fine baby-sitter, a young mother in the area who was willing to take care of any preschoolers right in her home during the study.

Of greatest significance, the Lord placed a prayer responsibility for this class upon a godly group of older women at our church. They prayed together. They prayed alone. And almost without fail, they prayed for us every Wednesday morning.

Often I would be asked by one of them, "How did things go on Wednesday? I prayed for you." It's hard work to pray, but "the earnest prayer of the righteous man has great power and wonderful results."[1]

---

[1]James 5:16 (*Living Letters*).

**Telling It
Like
It Is**

The fateful Wednesday came. We were excited and frightened, but our direction was set. Six women came. This meant three in addition to Nena, Marie and myself. I was a little disappointed that more of the "yes" phone responses hadn't shown up in person. Nevertheless, we had started.

We sat around the dining room table with a pot of coffee, sweet rolls, ashtrays for those who smoked, and our Bibles opened to the first chapter of Mark. Everyone brought her own Bible. For those who came without Bibles, we supplied free copies of *Good News for Modern Man.*[1] We read the chapter by paragraphs, and Marie asked questions—usually three basic ones: "What does it

[1] Published by American Bible Society (New York, 1966).

say?" "What does it mean?" and "What does it mean to me?"

In a few minutes we were enveloped in history, captivated by John the Baptist as he proclaimed a message of repentance, listening with the crowd as he introduced them to the most unique Man of them all, Jesus Christ. The familiar story came alive, and so did the conflict. Immediately one of the women said she could not accept the deity of Jesus Christ. It was a serious hang-up for her and it colored her response to what we read.

The natural inclination in a circumstance like this is to argue. But argument, no matter how well presented, seldom convinces anyone. In this situation nothing was resolved, at least not then. Perhaps the discussion ended in a draw, but the Scripture stood unchanged.

As women were added week by week to the group, it became even more evident that argument would win none of them. We had women from diverse religious backgrounds—Russian Orthodox, Roman Catholic and a wide swath of Protestant denominations. Even the women who were admittedly nonchurchgoers would still usually claim some sort of religious affiliation. They all had rather rigid ideas and philosophies. The common denominator, therefore, for this variant group was the Bible itself, though we didn't use any particular translation. Each woman brought the version she had. Whatever version was used, the Bible alone became the final authority for all of us.

It was fascinating to watch some who at first were highly opinionated, give way to the authority of Scripture. They learned not to argue as much or force their ideas on others. They learned to mentally weigh what they heard before speaking. One of the frequently asked questions was "Is that your opinion or is that actually what the Bible says?"

The Bible spoke with authority, it made an impact. We didn't have to defend it. And it was thrilling to see women begin to accept its authority in their lives.

One morning one of the ladies, following a lively discussion over a point that another person found difficult to accept, flatly declared, "It just boils down to whether you are going to believe what the Bible says or not. Me—I choose to accept it."

Some women couldn't accept it. They gradually stopped coming to the class. One of our active members ran into one such former study participant one day and asked her why she didn't come anymore. She replied, "As long as we were in the New Testament, it wasn't hard to believe what was said. But I just can't swallow Genesis, especially the hundreds of years people were supposed to have lived then." The first lady answered by her objection quite simply, "You can't believe only the parts of the Bible that you find convenient to believe. You either accept all of it or none of it. Maybe we don't understand all it says, but we can still believe it's true."

And so the lines were drawn. Persons constantly exposed to the Bible's truths could not remain impassive or indifferent or immune. We had to accept it or reject it.

The Bible's authority also provided a refuge for the leader when the passage under discussion covered touchy areas of daily living. It's easy enough to be quite impersonal about abstract doctrine. It's a lot harder to avoid the direct barbs of such statements as "Practice hospitality. Bless those who persecute you; bless and do not curse them. Live in harmony with one another; do not be haughty, but associate with the lowly. . . . Repay no one evil for evil. Practice hospitality. Show no partiality. . . . Let love be genuine."[2]

This penetrates to where I live. It affects my attitudes. It challenges my "rights" to live as I please. It demands involvement. And it hurts. We can sidestep the issues and say, "That doesn't apply to me." We can turn the message off completely and not even hear it. We can openly refuse to accept it. Or we can receive it and allow God to change our lives through it. The women in the Bible study did some or all of these things. When the study leader could sense resentment

[2]Rom. 12:14, 16-17, 13, 9. (RSV).

rising over a point that hit home, her comforting refuge lay in the fact that she could always say, "I didn't make that statement. God did. If you don't agree, discuss it with him."

Christ always spoke with authority. It upset the religious leaders of his day, but it attracted the crowds of ordinary people. He spoke their language, he related to them. His word had the same appeal for the women in the study.

One morning we were discussing marriage and divorce as it is found in Mark 10. The question was asked, "According to this passage what is God's plan for marriage?" Quickly the answer came:

"It was meant to be a permanent relationship in this life."

"What altered God's original intention?"

"Man's sin and stubborn refusal to accept God's plan."

"Whose work then is being destroyed by divorce?"

"God's."

One of the women in the group sat and listened, then asked, "But is there no way out? What do you do when your husband beats you?" This portion of the Bible hit her hard because her own marriage was so miserable. She would have preferred an easier release from a very hard situation.

On another occasion when this same chapter was being discussed someone asked, "How do you know that it is God who has joined together a man and woman in marriage? What if they were young kids and got drunk and got married under those conditions? Can you say 'God joined them'?" That question was batted around for quite a while! But we learned that the Bible doesn't let us off any hook too easily. God holds us individually responsible before him and we can't blame him for our irresponsible acts. In these real-life situations for which there were no pat answers, the Bible met the women where they lived; and even when they didn't always like what they read, they appreciated the authority with which it spoke.

The Bible study didn't build into a crowd overnight. We began with six. After the first session Marie left us on our own, and Nena and I alternated in leading the study. We kept in touch with the women between our get-togethers. It was hard for them to establish a new habit of setting aside one morning of the week because it meant rescheduling household tasks around Wednesday. But after about two months of working hard at it on the phone and in person, and fighting discouragement when the response was low, the study caught fire. Attendance shot up to twelve, fifteen and even eighteen.

The upsurge of interest was clearly not due to our "dynamic" personalities or "brilliant" discussion methods. Nena and I were both novices in this and we felt our way along with a great deal of prayer and reliance upon the Lord. Rather, it was the discovery by the women themselves that this book, which had gathered dust on a shelf in their homes because they had assumed it was too hard to understand, was not dead. It lived. It told them about life "like it really is." And when they became enthusiastic they invited their friends.

We ourselves became more excited as we realized anew that we were studying no mere philosophy, but the true living Word of God. The Old Testament Prophet Isaiah put it this way: "The grass withers, the flower fades, but the word of our God will stand for ever."[3]

[3]Isa. 40:7 (RSV).

# 7

## New Life
## for Rhoda

Rhoda worked as a ward clerk at a veteran's hospital. She was introduced to the Bible study through a co-worker of hers who happened to be a member of the class. After her first visit, her reaction was, "I've gone to church all my life and know absolutely nothing about the Bible. This is great!"

For two months she attended the class faithfully, soaking in all she could. Her desire for knowledge seemed insatiable. She couldn't get enough. Then, suddenly, her world began to fall apart.

On a routine x-ray required of all employees at the hospital, a spot was discovered on her lung. It was uncertain whether she had contracted tuberculosis or if it were cancer or some other type of lesion. She entered the hospital for tests.

Everyone in the Bible study group prayed. In fact, the prayer time (when we asked for requests before the study) became one of the most vital parts of the morning. Rhoda headed the list each Wednesday.

After two weeks of x-rays and other tests the diagnosis was still uncertain and surgery was scheduled. In spite of her hospitalization, Rhoda had followed the study in Mark. Each Wednesday afternoon I would phone her to tell her the highlights of the morning's discussion.

The day before her surgery, Liz, the friend who had brought her to the study, and I went to the hospital. We each had a preschooler in tow, so Liz went up to see Rhoda first while I baby-sat in the lobby. Liz told me later that during my visiting turn she prayed all the time while pulling our two children out of the "jungle" of potted palms. While alert for the necessary discipline and restraint of our offspring, she still maintained steady communion with God for Rhoda and for me. It was good she did. She was praying I would have the courage to say what had to be said.

Rhoda was in isolation. I put on a gown and mask before opening her door. The room was dismal. The windows were so grimy it was impossible to see out, and very little light came in. But her greeting was warm. She asked me right away about the most recent study in Mark. Then she told me she had been reading the Bible on her own. It had helped to pass the long hours of her day. But it had done more than that. She said, "In these two weeks of reading I have discovered I'm not as nice as people, or even I, may think I am." The Bible had become a mirror revealing not what other people saw but what she actually was in the eyes of God. A discovery like that is usually painful.

We talked about this for a while. Then I asked, "Have you ever committed your life to Jesus Christ?"

"No", she replied.

"Would you like to?"

"I certainly would."

Her reply was firm and unhesitating. We bowed our heads. Rhoda prayed first. I recall only one statement she made, "Lord, I submit my whole will to yours." Then I prayed. That bare, grim, hospital room was turned into a place to meet God. We sensed his presence.

When we raised our heads we were both in tears. It didn't matter what she had that might be contagious; I put my arms around her and kissed her through the mask. She was closer than a sister because Jesus Christ establishes a bond that surpasses even that of blood relations. I left the room reluctantly. Heaven was there.

The minute I stepped off the elevator into the lobby, Liz knew from one look at my face that a momentous transaction had occurred. The lobby was filled with busy activity, people coming and going, others sitting and waiting. We were totally unaware of them all as we stood in the middle of the room and wept tears of indescribable joy.

There is nothing in life which quite compares to the wonder and exultation of seeing a person born into the kingdom of God. And we got thoroughly emotional about it. It has always been difficult for me to understand why emotion is perfectly acceptable at a baseball game or in politics, but is considered suspect in spiritual experience. Liz and I walked out of the hospital with damp eyes but our feet seemed to float above the ground.

On the elevated train returning home, the doubts began to hit. I turned to Liz with a frightening thought, "What if I didn't go about it in the right way? What if she isn't saved after all?" And the questions kept tumbling out. I hadn't used any special set of Bible verses or followed the plans or procedures so carefully taught in personal evangelism classes. It scared me that I might have stumbled Rhoda, instead of helping her, by not using the right approach.

It was at this point the Lord stopped me cold, as this question came to my mind: *Winnie, since when do you save anyone? Redemption is my work and mine alone.* True. Relief poured in.

Redemption is God's work. He is not limited to a method. Neither is he limited to an individual. He is just nice enough to let us share in what he is doing once in a while. God was at work that day, and we had the unique privilege of seeing him work.

Rhoda went to surgery the following morning. The diagnosis—cancer. A lobe of her lung was removed and her prognosis was poor. She was a young woman with five young children. The doctor gave her the story straight. She knew her prospects for recovery were slim.

She was six days in the intensive-care unit. But as soon as she was moved to a ward, Liz and I went to see her. Again we took turns. I knew she would be physically very ill, but it was her morale I wondered about. I walked into her room, a much brighter place this time. She couldn't move too well because there were tubes inserted in her chest and attached to a pressure pump beneath her bed. She was weak, but her face glowed. She greeted me with "Winnie, this has been the most wonderful week in my life. It was like walking out of night into day." Only God could work a miracle like that.

Rhoda's postoperative recovery was painfully slow. Her lung didn't heal; it kept leaking air. She had a second operation and more lung tissue was removed, but still it wouldn't heal.

One afternoon Liz phoned to say Rhoda's doctor had passed the word that if her friends wanted to see her alive they had better go right then. My husband and I went to the hospital that evening. Rhoda looked more frail than ever but her face was serene. We didn't say much. She was too weak to talk. Chuck read a few verses from the Bible and prayed before we left. In the morning Rhoda was still there.

And all this time the women in the Bible study had prayed for her every Wednesday. Some of the new women had never met her and yet they prayed just as fervently as the rest of us. Rhoda was hospitalized eleven weeks and had three operations. Hope for her physical recovery had been given up. But God didn't let her die, and one morning in spring she came home.

The second Wednesday out of the hospital she was back at the Bible study. She still had a tube taped to her chest which made her arm movements awkward. She sat on the couch and said, "Being a Christian is so new to me. I have so much to learn. But it's great. I want to thank all of you for praying." Our prayer time that morning was filled with thanksgiving.

We had seen a double miracle in Rhoda, spiritual and physical. It was God's answer to our prayers for her that convinced many of the women that our Bible study had a "hot line" straight to heaven.

Two and a half years later, Rhoda is well. She works hard at home as well as assisting her husband in his business. In fact, her hard work and unwavering faith had a lot to do with bringing the business from the brink of failure to a successful, going concern. Rhoda is also a vocal soloist in her church. Her growth in the knowledge of the Bible brought her to that March morning when she led our study in Romans 10.

She said to me recently, "I realize that my life and everything I possess have been entrusted to me by the Lord to be used for him." This includes some vacation property she and her husband own in Wisconsin. She admitted she couldn't go up there without taking along at least one or two extra children who would otherwise never get out of the city. She gives of herself and her time selflessly to others, always cheerfully.

When God does a work, he does it well.

# 8

## God
## Versus
## the Mob

*Lord, I hadn't figured on taking on the syndicate too!* My cry was inaudible but very sincere. As the Bible study grew, it quickly emerged from an hour and half meeting one day a week to constant involvement with the women seven days a week. It was in these private sessions during the week, over the phone and in person, where the real problems came to light. It was here that we got behind the "lace curtain," as someone has effectively dubbed the protective veneer each woman so carefully builds around herself. The Bible study provided the framework for the personal contacts.

If availability was important in making friends it became paramount in maintaining the study. This morning it was Ellen who dropped by. She was fairly new to the group and full of questions.

How did the Bible study start? What was its purpose? etc. Slowly the ice was broken and we got down to the real reason for her visit.

I put away my vacuum cleaner and we sat down over a cup of coffee to talk. Ellen had been reared in a church-oriented home. As a child she had trusted Christ. But when she became a teen-ager she rebelled and her attitude of rebellion followed her right into marriage. She was independent. She was stubborn. And she and her husband were in trouble.

Her husband's line of work had involved him with the syndicate. To the person living outside its environs, the mention of Chicago often conjures up a picture of a metropolis in the clutches of gangsters. The average resident of Chicago looks at it more casually. While we are all well aware of corrupt business practices, loan sharks, bribery, rackets, extortion, con men and vice, usually these sinister words come no closer to us than newspaper articles. As her story unfolded the realization dawned on me that what had been merely a remote newspaper-type account before, was now being related as firsthand experience. I had heard of the tactics used by the mob when someone in their clutches didn't fall right in line with their wishes. They were masters at snaring and scaring innocent people. But that was all a million miles away from me; it couldn't happen so close to home.

Yet, here she sat telling me of the terror which crept up her back when the phone rang or when they ran into one of the "boys." And now a new dimension had been added. The law had caught up with this phase of illegal activity, and her husband faced trial.

Cold fear began to grip my stomach. I was being swept into involvement in an area where I wanted no involvement, so I cried silently to God. My fear was unreasonable and irrational. Fear often is. It can cripple us into inaction. But the more Ellen and I talked, the more the Lord seemed to take over, and a reasonable, inner calm replaced the fear. The crisis passed. God remained larger than the problem.

On the morning of the trial Ellen came to our home. We drank coffee. We talked. We prayed. It was hard to know how to pray. Her husband was guilty as charged and deserved punishment, but his family was innocent. Why should they suffer for the wrong he had done? An imprisonment or fine would hurt them all. We could only pray that the Lord would solve the problem for the best welfare of all concerned. And he did just that.

The hours of the morning seemed eternal. We kept watching the clock as the interminable minutes ticked by. Finally the scheduled hour of trial came and went. Ellen went home to wait for news of the outcome.

Because this was his first offense, her husband

was merely put on probation. He had to report to the authorities regularly. He couldn't travel freely for the duration of the probation. Thus the responsibility for his crime was put squarely on his shoulders, and his family was spared both the stigma of a criminal sentence and an expense which they could ill afford. The Lord had wonderfully answered prayer. But we didn't stop praying there.

It was Ellen's fervent desire for her husband to get out of that particular line of work altogether. He wasn't too deeply enmeshed in the syndicate's operation yet. He was still a small man in the total picture. But continued involvement could trap him to the point of no return, and the next brush with the law might have more dire results. So we kept praying.

In a very short while another job opportunity came her husband's way. This one was totally free of syndicate involvement. The Lord's answer was beyond our expectations.

Today Ellen admits that, though there is less money coming in, there is nothing which can compare to the freedom of walking out of her house and not having to look over her shoulder to see who is watching her movements, or tensing up every time the phone rings. The fat paychecks that reward illegal activities may be inviting, but they can't pay the cost of personal bondage and fear which always seem to accompany them. Ellen's observation bore out the truth of the Bible's statement that "the way of transgressors is hard."[1]

The whole Bible study group faced the reality of the syndicate later when one of our most faithful members didn't show up one Wednesday morning. She and her family had gone into hiding after a threatening phone call in the middle of the night. Her husband was a policeman who dared to be honest in his work and refused to be intimidated or bribed. In so doing he stepped on the toes of the syndicate, and, in typical fashion, they retaliated with threats to his family. Our most effective weapon in the situation was still prayer. And, believe me, we prayed.

Again the Lord answered. He protected the family from harm but, more than that, he kept their minds in peace. They were serene in the face of danger.

This mark of tranquillity has been in evidence in other areas as well. Several of the women in our Bible study had sons and daughters who attended a high school where riots and acts of violence were rather common for a while. Rhoda's son was jumped by fifteen boys on his way home from school one afternoon, and beaten. Police patrolled outside the school as well as the halls inside. With every upsetting incident the rumors grew to fantastic proportions. Parents panicked. Many felt

[1]Prov. 13:15.

the only solution was to run—move away—leave. The primary attitude in evidence in the Bible study group, however, was one of serenity. Quiet faith in Jesus Christ made a difference. They really believed the Lord was able to care for their children. Rhoda was grateful her son wasn't severely hurt, and he returned to school the following day as though nothing had happened. One mother whose daughter is a freshman this year said the other day, "I'm in absolute peace about it. The Lord is watching over her."

The syndicate and a rise in violence represent only two of the many enemy strongholds operating in the world about us. All too often Christian people view these strongholds as imperishable giants. And so, when we are confronted by these giants, our response is to run, to refuse to get involved, or to think, *If I don't see it, it's not really there.* This naive, head-in-the-sand attitude is more prevalent than it should be.

So Christians, as individuals and as members of a church, often spend more time and energy building defenses than in actively trying to penetrate enemy territory. That would be too dangerous. Yet the description Christ gave of his church was not of a defensive organism, but an aggressive one. He said, "I will build my church; and the gates of hell shall not prevail against it."[2] This is a

[2]Matt. 16:18.

church on the move, not one standing still. When the church in Jerusalem didn't spread out as the Lord had told it to, he allowed persecution to come and sting the believers into moving. Perhaps the Lord is repeating the pattern today.

The Lord doesn't expect us to be reckless or foolish in our zeal. But he does expect us to get involved with people right where they live and to rely on him for the courage we need from day to day. The pattern should be like David's. In the course of his daily work as a shepherd, a bear and a lion threatened the sheep. David killed them. He later remembered these experiences as deliverances by the hand of God. Then one day he faced a human giant.

If anyone had told him that morning, as he set out to take food to his soldier brothers, that in the evening he would return home with the head of a giant, he probably wouldn't have believed it. But that's exactly what happened. The God who had been powerful enough to help him overcome in the daily crises of life, was also great enough to cope with the giant. It was not the magnitude of the situation which struck him. It was the magnitude of his God which motivated him.

If we dared to trust the Lord from day to day and draw our strength from him to meet each problem as it comes, refusing to run in fear or to be intimidated, then we too would see more giants crumble. The Lord hasn't given us a "spirit of timidity but a spirit of power and love and self-control."[3]

Moses encouraged his people with these words when they faced a formidable array of enemies: "Be strong and of good courage, do not fear . . . for it is the LORD your God who goes with you; he will not fail you or forsake you."[4]

The same God is with us today. It's about time we trusted him.

[3]II Tim. 1:7 (RSV).
[4]Deut. 31:6 (RSV).

# 9

## Dead Leaves

The Bible study had been going about five months.
As the numbers grew, Nena had added leaves to
her dining room table until it was fully extended.
One particular morning every seat around the table
was filled and there was an overflow semicircle of
four or five women. We were still alternating in
leading and it was my turn. Nena sat with the
overflow group on a chair near the kitchen door.
She was unusually quiet that morning. She didn't
participate in the discussion and she really looked
miserable. I thought she was ill. There were several
occasions when she had had the flu or a sinus
headache on a Wednesday morning, but she
refused to give in to either and determinedly went
through with her role as Bible study hostess. Then
she would collapse in the afternoon. But today her

problem wasn't due to a virus or a bad headache.

The Bible study progressed as usual. There was plenty of lively participation, but I was very much aware of my "silent partner." Following the study there was little opportunity for private conversation as most of us had to hurry to be home before our children returned from school for lunch. Consequently, it wasn't until the middle of the afternoon that Nena and I got together by phone.

She opened the conversation. "You knew there was something wrong this morning, didn't you?"

"Yes, I thought you were sick. Are you all right?"

"Oh, I'm fine, not sick, that is. It's something else. The Lord was talking to me this morning about my smoking. I've been battling with him ever since. This afternoon while cleaning the bedroom, I gave up the fight. I knelt down and turned my life, without reservation, over to God. You know, Winnie, for me cigarettes were a symbol of inner rebellion against the Lord. I didn't control those cigarettes. They controlled me. It's amazing what a slave I was to a weed and piece of paper. I don't want anything to control me more than Christ. So, as of this afternoon, I have stopped smoking!"

For Nena, this was a major crisis in her life. It was a battle fought and won by the Lord.

We had purposely not made an issue of smoking in the Bible study. In fact, we tried not to be negative about anything. Comments made later by some of the women revealed what an important factor this proved to be in the appeal the study had for them.

Several women had been exposed to rigid "fundamentalist" backgrounds. One woman said that her church had emphasized that it was "the things that you *don't* do that make you a good Christian."

Another woman frankly admitted that had she known at the beginning that I had the slightest fundamentalist connections she wouldn't have come. Some dogmatic, opinionated young Christians had tried to argue her into the kingdom of God and had turned her off completely. Fortunately, she was "hooked" on the Bible study before she made the "damaging" discovery that my husband worked for a Christian organization.

Dan Piatt, who trains counselors for Billy Graham's crusades, gave a very helpful illustration in one of his training sessions several years ago. He spoke of the various trees in the fall season whose leaves turn brown and fall off. An exception was the oak tree. The oak tree's leaves will often hang on all through the winter. And it's not until the spring when the new life surges through the tree that those old dead leaves will finally be pushed off as new fresh leaves replace them. He used this as an illustration of a new Christian. He pointed out that older Christians often get more anxious to cut off the "old leaves" of bad habits in a new believer than they are to feed the new life within. He said, "You feed that new life and nourish it and you won't have to worry about the dead leaves. They'll just fall off by themselves."

This is what we tried to do in the study—to be positive—to present Christ, and approach the Scriptures simply, honestly, and objectively. And if there were "negatives" to be presented, to trust the Spirit of God to make the application in individual lives. It was an approach which apparently worked, for one of the women later commented, "My first impression was that the teaching would be too narrow-minded. My impressions changed because instead of sins being the number-one important lesson learned, it was the love of God."

This was the lesson which touched Nena. From the very beginning she had smoked as she led the study. Not a word was said. But I'll admit it was a subject of personal prayer! Nena showed herself to be such an effective leader and good teacher that I personally felt that she would hinder the scope of her outreach if she remained captive to smoking. However, if I had told her she couldn't lead and smoke at the same time, one of two things might have resulted—she could have become resentful and closed herself to usefulness, or she might have tried to stop to please me. This would have been such a shallow reason that it wouldn't have lasted.

By waiting for the Lord to do the work, the job was done far better. And it was permanent.

The decision to quit smoking as an act of total submission to Jesus Christ was a crisis. It was followed by a process which was no easier than the original crisis had been. Anyone who has stopped smoking will testify to the definite physical withdrawal symptoms besides the terrific craving for "just one more before I quit."

My next-door neightbor, another member of the Bible study, had stopped smoking about three years earlier and had a keen awareness of what Nena would go through. With this in mind she prepared a "survival kit" with beautifully wrapped packages of toothpicks, life savers, gum, aspirin, all marked to be opened right after breakfast, 10 A.M., after lunch, after dinner, bedtime, or, "when you think you can't last another minute!" We also phoned Nena at regular intervals to encourage her or dropped in to see her. And we prayed.

The first twenty-four hours were the worst. Nena paced the floor, chewed dozens of tooth-picks, went to prayer meeting Wednesday evening "just to get out of the house right after supper." She was so nervous she was ready to climb the walls.

Then Friday morning she phoned. "Well, I'm free! The Lord delivered me and I'm at peace." It wasn't that she would never be tempted to smoke again, but the awful struggling seemed to be over.

Bill Anderson, a teacher at Emmaus Bible School, defined this sort of Christian experience in this way: "The Spirit of God will give me enough help to get the job done, but not enough so that there will be no struggle. He'll make it possible but not without a contest."

The disciplines of the Christian life are not meant to be easy. Victorious Christian living does not mean "no sweat." It does mean, though, that in the conflict we have available all the resources of God himself, not to barely get us through but to bring us through in triumph.

The impact of Nena's experience with the Lord was immediately evident in the group. She was a released person. There was added reality in her approach to the Bible because we knew that God had spoken to her and changed her through it.

Then one of the women faced her with a prickly question "What are you going to say when people ask you why you have stopped smoking?"

"You did have to ask that, didn't you?" Nena retorted. "How about if I said that I didn't want to get lung cancer?"

"Was that the reason?" asked her friend.

"No, of course not," replied Nena. "None of those warnings ever scared me into quitting."

"I guess you had better be honest then," was the quiet reply.

The test of "honesty" came that first weekend when Nena entertained the monthly meeting of a community women's group in her home. These were women from the community drawn together by one basic common interest—nursing babies— and most of them smoked. Nena awaited the first comment nervously. The women gathered, chatted enthusiastically about their babies, lit their cigarettes, and no one even noticed that Nena hadn't joined them in the latter activity!

After letting a period of time go by, Nena couldn't stand it any longer, so she called for the floor. "Didn't anyone notice that I'm not smoking?" she asked. Well, no, no one had noticed. The ladies looked at her with curiosity to see what would follow. Nena proceeded to explain that God had done for her what she couldn't do for herself. She told them that her greatest desire was to be totally controlled by Jesus Christ.

This was puzzling language for some of them, but they resumed their conversation in more subdued tones, and Nena noticed that within two minutes every cigarette in the room had been snuffed out.

One of her friends commented, "You'll last six weeks and then be back with the rest of us."

Another said, "You'll go back to it. You'll get over your religious fling and revert to your old ways."

But Nena's reply was, "If I were depending on my own power, you would be right. But the Lord is doing this, and it's permanent." This didn't make her friends feel particularly comfortable.

As women came to know the Lord in the Bible study group, we didn't make smoking an issue in their lives. But the Lord did, and when he started to work, someone would come up with a "survival kit" to help the person along, and our own circle of "smokers anonymous" developed.

There are women, however, who continue to smoke and who are continuing in their growth in the knowledge of Christ and his Word. For them, it is a futile exercise to try to hack off the brown leaves on their own. One woman tried this because she began to feel "out of it" when others had stopped smoking. It didn't work for her, and when she returned to it she felt guilty and tried to hide it. It became a thoroughly oppressive situation until she accepted the fact that she just couldn't stop smoking at that point.

Having made the admission, she turned her attention to studying the Bible again and learning of Christ, and has been a lot happier since. The Lord hasn't convicted her and we don't condemn her.

The individual whose life is firmly rooted in Jesus Christ and who is nourished by his Word and walks in obedience to it *will* show outward evidence of that inner life.

The psalmist expressed it like this: "Blessed is the man who walks not in the counsel of the wicked, nor stands in the way of sinners, nor sits in the seat of scoffers; but his delight is in the law of the LORD, and on his law he meditates day and night. He is like a tree planted by streams of water, that yields its fruit in its season, and its leaf does not wither. In all that he does, he prospers."[1]

For Nena, the way to this state of perpetual spring was opened the day she allowed the Lord to take full control of her life, even of her smoking.

[1]Ps. 1:1-3 (RSV).

**10**

**To Lead
is
to Learn**

When the Bible study consistently overflowed into a second circle around Nena's dining room table, we decided to break down into two smaller groups, one remaining in the dining room, the other in the recreation room. The women drew numbers as they came in Wednesday morning to determine which group they would be in. This kept the groups mixed up each week, but it also meant that both Nena and I had to lead each week.

At this point we decided that some of the women who had been coming regularly were ready to take a crack at leading. We tried not to force anyone, but we used determined persuasion! In some Bible studies, everyone wants to lead. In ours, no one was all that eager. But with persistent prodding we finally worked in two or three more leaders. More were added as the year progressed.

Although we were using the study guide *Mark*, and after that the book *Acts*,[1] we encouraged the women to essentially do their own studying in the chapter first. This meant reading the chapter over several times, perhaps even ten or twenty times, reading it in different translations, then writing down the important facts in the chapter and what meaning it had for them personally. Bible commentaries, such as *The Wycliffe Bible Commentary* or *The New Bible Commentary*, or *Matthew Henry's Commentary* and a good Bible dictionary, as well as the study guides, are all useful tools in Bible study. But what makes a discussion vibrant is what has become meaningful in the life of the person leading and those responding.

I would far rather hear a leader communicate one truth which has gripped her own heart in her study, than to listen to her relating ten profound statements, gleaned from a commentary, which are virtually meaningless to her. We also avoid bringing commentaries to the study, as reading from one seems to have a deadening effect on discussion. Since our Bible studies are based on questions, the study guides were especially helpful in framing the questions to bring out the most important facts.

[1] Published by Neighborhood Bible Studies, Inc. (Dobbs Ferry, N.Y., 1961).

To be an effective Bible study leader means taking time in preparation. This means bringing out of storage old study habits which may not have been used since school days and perhaps establishing a few new ones as well. In one situation Nena spent seven hours helping a new leader pull the meaning out of a chapter verse by verse. It was a grueling ordeal, after which the woman exclaimed, "I had no idea leading took this much preparation! When *you* do it, it seems as easy as rolling off a log!"

The fact that study takes time should never hinder anyone from leading, however. We take time and make time for all kinds of projects and ventures which interest us, and none of them are as rewarding as time spent in the study of the Bible. You never "waste" time doing this and it's time well invested.

Two sisters in the New Testament periodically had Jesus as a guest in their home. Mary made it her practice to sit and listen to Jesus' teaching. Martha, her sister, resented the time Mary spent doing this. But Jesus defended her, saying, "Mary has chosen the good portion, which shall not be taken away from her."[2] Both the privilege of listening and the time so spent were a secure investment paying permanent dividends. No other investment offers such security. The Old Testa-

[2] Luke 10:42 (RSV).

ment Prophet Isaiah declared quite simply, "The word of our God will stand for ever."[3]

Over and over again the women who led said, "I get so much more out of it when I lead." And many of the women continued on their own in taking Bible correspondence courses from Moody Bible Institute or Emmaus Bible School to gain insight in the Scriptures and to establish better study habits. I'm afraid television soap operas lost some faithful viewers as these women revised the use of their time.

A leader needs to be enthusiastic. If the subject isn't exciting to her, it won't be to anyone else either. She also should be flexible. If the discussion goes in an unplanned direction (and it usually does), it's very possible that the question being raised is of greater importance at the moment than the planned questions.

For example, a recent discussion revolved around the statement, "Render to Caesar the things that are Caesar's, and to God the things that are God's."[4] One of the women said, "I stayed awake most of last night trying to delineate what was Caesar's and what was God's as it related to my involvement in the community."

This discussion lasted for an hour. It was important. It was relevant to all of us.

[3]Isa. 40:8 (RSV).
[4]Mark 12:17 (RSV).

However, the leader also needs to bring the discussion back on course if it gets too far afield. Discerning what is a needful discussion and what is just an unnecessary tangent takes experience, and a good knowledge of the women involved.

Flexibility is also necessary when a leader, scheduled to take the study, calls up ill the day before. Another leader has to fill in on short notice. Instead of moaning over the short time for preparation, she just goes ahead and does it. The Lord seems to stand by with an extra supply of strength for situations like that.

Another helpful asset for a leader is to be "shock proof." Some people just enjoy testing another person's "shock level," even by using profanity, especially if they feel that individual has lived a sheltered life. Others are just completely themselves and in discussions will come out with exactly what's on their minds.

One morning the subject being discussed was Jesus' betrayal and arrest in the Garden of Gethsemane. We tried to put ourselves in the places of the disciples on that fateful occasion, tried to imagine what went through their minds, why they all forsook Jesus and fled. We were thoroughly absorbed in the story when one of the women suggested, "I can just imagine those disciples seeing that crowd coming armed with clubs and swords, saying to each other, 'Well, fellas, this doesn't look too good for us. Let's get the hell out of here!' " After a brief moment of stunned silence everyone burst out laughing. It really wasn't too difficult to imagine someone like Peter, the rough coarse fisherman who had a habit of putting his tongue in motion ahead of his mind, saying something exactly like that.

In another Bible study King Herod was tagged "a real swinger"!

Women enjoyed discovering that Bible people were similar to people today. They had the same weaknesses, the same problems, the same reactions, the same emotions. Because they could identify with Bible characters like this, it made it easier for them to relate Bible solutions to their lives and problems as well. Then there are always those who refuse to let the Bible relate to them, as one lady flatly declared in our study one morning, "I don't care what the Bible says, you'll never convince me on that point!"

Women need to voice their doubts and questions, no matter how startling, without fear of being shot down for their ideas. We must respect each person for what she is, just as she is.

A leader shouldn't demand immediate acceptance of the things she says. We share the Bible, plant the seed, but the Holy Spirit is the one who makes it grow. We don't help his work by overwatering and overcultivating. It doesn't hurt for a leader to develop a tough skin too. She can't afford to be touchy and sensitive when barbs are shot her way. She needs to field criticisms, diversity of opinion without taking it personally, yet, at the same time remain sensitive to the feelings of others. Think that's impossible? You're right! It takes the supernatural working of God in our lives to produce in us what we can't produce ourselves.

Sometimes the "tough hide" is helpful when there is no comment at all. A leader appreciates encouraging reactions afterward, but if they're not forthcoming it takes an extra dose of faith to leave the study in the hands of God (where it belongs anyway) and not to consider herself a total failure. Even if she does fluff a study one morning (and it's bound to happen) she picks up and goes on, hopefully learning by the experience.

A sense of humor is always an asset. My father, who was a missionary to the Orient for over 50 years, used to say that there were two necessary ingredients for being a good missionary: a good sense of humor, and no sense of smell! Certainly the aspect of humor helps in a Bible study too. A leader shouldn't take herself too seriously and should be able to laugh at herself and at her mistakes. The world really isn't going to stand or fall on what we do or say or don't do or don't say at a given time. If we honestly and sincerely seek to walk in fellowship with the Lord, do our part in preparation as best as possible, and turn the study over to him in prayer, then the burden of responsibility for the results belong to the Lord.

Humor helps to relieve pressure when it builds up in the group or in us as individuals. The pressure of being perpetual hostess to the Bible study would get to Nena once in a while, especially if she had sick children or wasn't well herself. I would frequently suggest to her that we move it to my home for a while, but her usual reply was "Nope. I want that Bible study to meet in my home until I can honestly say some Wednesday morning, when I'm sitting at a chaotic breakfast table, rushing to get the children off to school, 'Thank God all those women are coming to my house in two hours!' "

"Well," I laughed, "I guess the Bible study is a permanent fixture at your house then!"

A leader also has to develop a sense of responsibility. This means faithfulness in attending whether it's her turn to lead or not. This, perhaps, may seem like an unnecessary comment, but we have found that a commitment to responsibility is a missing dimension in many areas of Christian service today. If an opportunity to do something more interesting comes at a time conflicting with our responsibility the temptation is very strong to choose that which is more attractive at the moment. Constancy in responsibility marks a godly person; as the psalmist says, it is he "who swears to his own hurt and does not change."[5] We were

[5] Ps. 15:4 (RSV).

fortunate to have leaders who were committed to their responsibility. They came in the worst of weather and sometimes led in hoarse whispers when afflicted with laryngitis!

Faithfulness to a responsibility, no matter how insignificant the job may be, is a quality which the Lord recognizes and honors. A sense of responsibility also applies to a leader's concern for the other women during the week. She phones or visits or perhaps takes along a helpful book suited to a woman's particular need or problem. Our leaders became regular patrons of Christian bookstores to get materials to give out when needed.

A sense of despondency after leading a study was also a frequent occurrence. This shouldn't be surprising as it is evidence that we're engaged in spiritual conflict. Some mornings when we could sense the presence of the Holy Spirit in a marked way during the study, the temptation to discouragement would be even stronger after it.

Our experience along this line was small compared to that of Samson. On one occasion, in the power of the Spirit of God, he slew a thousand men with the jawbone of an ass. Immediately after this phenomenal victory, he was very thirsty, and he called on the Lord and said, "Thou hast granted this great deliverance by the hand of thy servant; and shall I now die of thirst, and fall into the hands of the uncircumcised?" He was so exhausted that he was sure his weakness would make him ready prey for his enemies. The Lord didn't rebuke him for his lack of faith, but he split open a hollow place "and there came water from it; and when he [Samson] drank, his spirit returned, and he revived."[6]

This same principle was the repeated experience of a missionary I heard of recently. Miss Victoria Christianson is her name and she went to India in 1922. A few years ago, after her retirement from active missionary work, she spoke at a missionary conference and told this story:

When she had gone out to India the first time, her church had prepared letters for her to open each day on board ship as she crossed the ocean. In this group of letters was one envelope marked to be opened "when you are discouraged with your progress."

It wasn't long after she had reached India, with its language and culture so foreign to her, that she became discouraged. She pulled out the letter; but then this thought came to her: *No human being can take the place of the Lord Jesus Christ.*

It was inconceivable to her that any person on earth could be better equipped to encourage her when she was down than the Lord himself. So she took her Bible, got on her knees and received strength from the Lord. The letter remained unopened.

[6]Judges 15:15-19 (RSV).

After a long life of service for God and many discouragements, she was now retired, and before that conference audience she triumphantly waved an envelope, yellowed with age, but still unopened. God had never let her down.

At the time of this writing I heard that Miss Christianson was living in our area in a retirement home, so I phoned her. I asked her if that letter were still unopened. She laughed and said, "Oh, yes. The discouragements still come, and every once in a while the Lord challenges me with that letter. But it helps me never to forget that my power is in Jesus Christ and him alone." She had learned the secret, as Samson had learned it, of true spiritual vitality.

For Bible study leaders the same problems of spiritual exhaustion, discouragement and despondency are very real. The temptation for us may not be to open a letter, but to pick up the phone and talk to a good friend. Christian friends are wonderful and can be very helpful, but they are never an adequate substitute for the Lord himself. It is vital for a leader, and for all Christians for that matter, to learn the secret of waiting alone before God to receive straight from him the strength, encouragement and vibrancy which only he can give.

Another practical suggestion is to invest in the longest phone cord the telephone company will install. From my own experience it's a great frustration saver. The necessary hours of phone counseling will not be "wasted" time when you can do dishes, scrub floors, fix meals, etc., while talking on the phone. In fact, I rarely carry on a phone conversation sitting down. Our phone cord allows me to work in four rooms. And my children have taken the cue from me. They don't work while conversing, but they wouldn't think of sitting next to the phone to talk. They go around a corner, stretch the cord to its limit, *then* find a chair to sit and talk!

The thought of "counseling" shouldn't frighten anyone, either. Professional counselors and pastors admit that the greatest percentage of their time is spent in listening. Leaders learn to be good listeners. Then, as they learn more of the Bible themselves they can often give answers based on scriptural principles. The Bible has a basic principle that parallels each of man's basic needs. This means that a leader has to learn for herself what the Bible says. A daily "quiet time" is essential.

An insidious danger to beware of is the presence of a competitive spirit which can arise between leaders. The Apostle Paul's remedy applies here: "Be humble toward each other, never thinking you are better than others. And look out for each other's interests, not for your own intersts."[7]

[7]Phil. 2:3-4 (*Good News for Modern Man*).

A leader needs to be careful not to overestimate her own importance, especially if she is the one who started a study group and feels, "This is my baby." If it is God's work, he will carry it on with or without a particular leader.

A leader, finally, should have just enough insecurity to make her totally dependent on the Lord. If we ever approach a study with the attitude "Boy, am I ever going to knock 'em dead this morning!" then we're lost before we've started. Because we came to recognize that without the help of the Lord all our efforts were wasted time and energy, we met together regularly for prayer.

Every Tuesday our leaders met to pray and to give themselves and the study into the Lord's hands. We knew that all the hours of study preparation and the use of the slickest teaching techniques would be sterile unless God was there and did the work. Our prayer was the key to his power. But we had to be careful not to let our prayer times deteriorate into "gossip sessions." The idea that we need to know all the intimate details about a person's problem "so we can pray more intelligently" is often a high-sounding excuse for our natural nosiness!

In a very practical sense the prayer time meant another morning of the week was "shot." We had to schedule other jobs around *two* mornings now. But it meant a firm commitment to its necessity, and every woman involved was convinced that prayer was vital. We prayed not only for ourselves but for everyone in the Bible study by name. And God worked.

The experiment of two Bible study groups meeting in the same house didn't last long because the women preferred to be all together. However, the split group did give the opportunity for new leaders to develop. They got used to leading in a smaller circle and then, when we combined into one again, the task didn't seem so formidable.

Small discussion groups are certainly preferable, but at this point there was no natural way to make the breakdown, so we just kept going as we were.

Each Bible study group develops its own personality. It will never be exactly like another group, and it shouldn't try to be. The complaint may arise, "But so and so doesn't do it that way." Well, too bad! We can learn from the experience of others but we limit the Lord if we confine him to only one method or one course of study or one personality.

Another technique we have recently stumbled on is to involve each member of the group by having each one lead the discussion of one paragraph. Asking leading questions about three or four verses isn't half so mountainous or frightening as doing the same for a whole chapter. We found it to be a rather painless way of "breaking in" potential leaders.

Our Bible study was not run democratically. This may have bordered on political heresy, but it worked anyway! We didn't vote on what we would study next. It wasn't that we ignored the desires of the women who came. The leaders listened to them, tried to see what were their greatest needs, prayed, made a choice, and followed through in faith. When we went to Genesis after Mark and Acts, many felt it was a mistake (especially some of the leaders, who groaned at all the study it would entail); but in Genesis Meg became a Christian. She is now leader of her own group.

The choosing of study materials and the method of study were widely varied. When we studied Genesis, all the leaders took the correspondence course on Genesis from Moody Bible Institute. But the Bible study was still conducted in the format of questions which the leader gleaned from her own study.

In some groups everyone takes a correspondence course. Some have made use of Shirley Rice's tapes and book *The Christian Home* and have found this very helpful. The leaders have to be prayerfully aware of the needs of the group and choose the subject of study accordingly.

Some groups find it helpful to have a secretary to keep the ladies informed as to whose turn it is to bring sweet rolls (always a voluntary chore), whose turn it is to lead, and in whose home the study will be meeting. Many groups rotate month by month from home to home. When it's at your house it's a great way to get your housework done!

We were learners together as leaders in the Bible study, and we're still learning. It gave us a fresh appreciation of the Apostle Paul's statement, "I was with you in weakness and in much fear and trembling; and my speech and message were not in plausible words of wisdom, but in demonstration of the Spirit and power, that your faith might not rest in the wisdom of men but in the power of God."[8]

[8] I Cor. 2:3-5 (RSV).

# 11

**Husbands Wanted!**

The first year of the Bible study closed in June with a progressive dinner to which the husbands were invited. Some of the husbands who were reluctant to participate in an event involving total strangers, were "prayed there" by their wives. Others were motivated by enough curiosity to meet this "Wednesday group" about which most of them had heard every Wednesday during dinner for months. Others chose not to come, but their wives came anyway.

The "entertainment" for the evening was a panel discussion on the first eleven chapters of Genesis, dealing with such general subjects as creation, evolution, and science and religion. The subject was picked by the ladies as something which would most interest their husbands in the Bible. The panel members included Phil Clarkson, a Christian businessman, and Dr. Alan Johnson, a teacher at Moody Bible Institute. The husbands found themselves getting involved in the discussion in spite of themselves, and Dr. Johnson remained to answer questions long after the discussion was officially ended.

Enough interest was aroused that evening for my husband to conduct an evening Bible study for men the following year.

Somehow the general feeling seems to be that religion is fine for women—"They're more emotional anyway and need that kind of stuff"—but for a man, commitment to faith seems to denote a loss of his masculine independence. Christianity, in particular, demands an acknowledgment that I'm not capable of saving myself, I'm not capable in myself to shape my own destiny, I must depend entirely on the work someone else, namely Jesus Christ, has done for me, to get where I want to go and to achieve the highest goals in life. And what man really wants to make admissions like that? He is supposed to be self-sufficient, ambitious, and perfectly capable of making his own way in life with help from no one.

The "typical" American male is pictured as a rugged individualist. From early childhood he walks with head unbowed. As a little boy he's not supposed to cry when punched in the nose. That would be a sign of weakness. Instead he practices delivering forceful punches himself because "no one is going to push me around!" As a teen-ager he would rather die of exhaustion than admit defeat on the basketball floor. As a university student he fights against "the establishment" perhaps because there are no other frontiers on which he can express his pioneering spirit. He doesn't have to fight for physical survival so, to give expression to his rugged individualism, he tries to destroy the protective hothouse in which he has been reared. As an adult he claws his way up the ladder of success (his rung is almost always determined by the size of his salary), totally disregarding those he may be stepping on to achieve his goals.

The setting for the development of this independent male is often a home which has provided financial security and the opportunity for the development of a heady freedom in which the parents have said, "I'll give my boy the best so he won't have to struggle like I did." Unfortunately, a life free of struggle is about the worst thing a parent can give a child.

When it comes to marriage this typical American male devotes most of his strength to his work. This is the primary outlet for maintaining his "rugged individualism." He strives for enough financial success to maintain his sense of independence so that he can truly feel that he is master of his own destiny as well as his family's. This commitment to independence tends to desensitize his conscience toward the finer qualities of mercy, truth and love. These qualities are expected of his wife, who must also assume the moral and spiritual responsibilities of the household.

Consequently we have a two-headed monster, one head being the rugged male in command of his destiny and the other a society which is essentially matriarchal because it is the woman who runs the house and everything else pertaining to the family.

Introduce Jesus Christ into this picture and the applecart is violently upset. For Jesus says, "If any man would come after me, let him deny himself and take up his cross and follow me."[1] There is humiliation in such identification. Many retreat from such self-deprecation because their views of Jesus Christ are distorted.

They think of him as a weak man because of his meekness. His humble beginnings didn't give him prestige. As far as we know he didn't own property or accumulate a bank account. He would never have made the news in the society pages. And yet he was every inch a man. He dominated the scene. Around him gathered a group of rugged men whose living was made by physical brawn, also slick businessmen, who in ordinary life would have been on opposite sides politically, and yet they worked together in harmony under Jesus'

[1] Matt. 16:24 (RSV).

leadership. It took a strong man to do that.

Jesus was no less a man because he was loving and patient with children, tender with the sick and elderly, and overcome with sorrow when he wept beside a grave. He could also wield a stinging whip when the occasion demanded it. The religious rulers of his day didn't scare him even when they threatened his life. He refused to be intimidated. He was a full-orbed man, and yet he lived a life of total submission to the will of his Father.

For most men the idea of submitting their wills to the will of Jesus Christ is both foreign and distasteful. It would be, to them, a sign of personal weakness. The husbands whose wives were in the Bible study group were no different than most. They were hard-working men, some of whom accepted condescendingly the religious interests of their wives, but they backed off if it demanded involvement for them. Their responsibility began and ended with providing a regular paycheck for their families. Any further demands would have been an infringement of their personal freedom.

The Bible cuts right through the two-headed monsters of our culture and gives us God's pattern for the Christian household. Christ is the head. Under him come the men in a position of subjection, dependence and personal commitment to him. They in turn are to be the heads of their homes. Whether they recognize the fact or not, God holds all men responsible not only for the physical and material well-being of their families but for the spiritual climate of their homes as well. Next in line come the wives in a position of submission to their husbands, and children are ordered to obey their parents. This order of affairs is clearly laid down in Ephesians 5 by the Apostle Paul. Where Christ is head of the home and the husband committed to him, it's not hard for the wife to submit nor for the children to obey, for the love of God permeates the whole scene.

The dilemma arises when a wife commits her life to Christ, but her husband couldn't care less about God's order of anything, or actually fights against his wife's desires and spiritual concerns.

One woman in the Bible study fairly shrieked at me one day, "You tell me to have faith. How do I have faith when my husband has his hands around my throat trying to choke the life out of me?"

Another time a woman quoted her husband as saying to her, "Nobody needs you around here! You belong in a state institution." Her question: "How do I love someone who screams this at me all day?"

Some husbands won't allow their wives any associations which would encourage spiritual development. One husband regularly disconnected wires in his car engine to keep his wife from going to a Bible study by car. Such oppressive domination reveals a basic insecurity. Such men don't want to be proved wrong. The interesting phenomenon is that when Jesus Christ enters a home it is very difficult for the rest of the family to remain completely indifferent. As one of our women described it, "You become someone else's conscience without even trying. It's unavoidable."

It was this dilemma of a divided household that brought Wilma to our home one morning. The coffee was poured, but hardly touched. She was too upset. Her body shook as she sobbed, "I'm no good to anyone. I'm a liability to my family. My husband says in the last eight months I've ruined our marriage. He said, 'You've changed, and I don't like what you've become.' What makes it really hurt is that I know it isn't true. I've been a much *better* wife and mother in these last eight months than I have been in ten years. Oh, I wish I were dead!"

Her husband's conscience had been activated by the change in her, but his ego wouldn't allow him to admit that she was a better person. So his defensive tactic was to assail her with accusations.

To get the pressure of conviction off himself, he tried to "knock down" the character of the person who was sensitizing his conscience. A lot of us do that. We think we can make ourselves look better by making someone else look worse, so we'll say, "Oh, she's all right I guess, *but—*" and then will follow a criticism of that person's weakness or bad habit which certainly "isn't true of me!"

No wonder the Bible says "The heart is deceitful above all things, and desperately wicked. Who can know it?"[2] We don't even recognize the rancid hypocrisy lying just inside our own heart's door.

That tactic is as old as the Garden of Eden. When God confronted Adam with his disobedience, Adam's first reaction was to point an accusing finger at his wife and say, "It's all *her* fault."

The Spirit of God was pointing a finger at Wilma's husband, bringing conviction of his own inadequacy. Fine. We recognized what was going on. But how was Wilma going to survive while her husband struggled? How does any woman live through a spiritually incompatible marriage?

The Apostle Peter had the answer. From the way he wrote in his first letter we would gather that this was not an uncommon dilemma in his day. This is what he wrote: "If you endure suffering even when you have done right, God will bless you for it. It was to this that God called you; because Christ himself suffered for you and left you an example, so that you would follow in his steps . . . . When he was cursed he did not answer back with a curse; when he suffered he did not threaten, but placed his hopes in God, the righteous Judge . . . . *In the same way you wives must*

[2] Jer. 17:9

*submit yourselves to your husbands,* so that if some of them do not believe God's word, they will be won over to believe by your conduct. It will not be necessary for you to say a word, for they will see how pure and reverent your conduct is .... You beauty should consist of your true inner self, the ageless beauty of a gentle and quiet spirit, which is of great value in God's sight. For in this way the devout women of the past, who hoped in God, used to make themselves beautiful, they submitted themselves to their husbands. Sarah was like that; she obeyed Abraham and called him 'My master.' You are now her daughters if you do good and are not afraid of anything."[3]

The key to living with an incompatible marriage situation is submission. Christ is given as the prime example of such submission. He endured unjust treatment in silence and without retaliation because he "placed his hopes in God, the righteous Judge."[4]

In exactly the same way, wives are to submit to their husbands. Submission doesn't always mean suffering, except that for some women (perhaps most) learning to keep their mouths shut is suffering! For the Christian woman with a non-Christian husband, submission is an attitude developed as she too learns "to set her hope in God."

[3]I Peter 2:20–3:6 (*Good News for Modern Man*).
[4]I Peter 2:23 (*Good News for Modern Man*).

Peter points to the godly women of past generations, and lifts out Sarah as an example to be emulated. The overriding pattern of her life was one of submission and obedience to her husband. I can hear some women saying, "Big deal! What wife wouldn't gladly submit to a man like Abraham? He was a man of tremendous faith in God. In fact he was called 'a friend of God.' If my husband were like that you'd better believe I'd submit to him."

It's true that Abraham was a giant of the faith, but he was also human and made some costly mistakes. When he left his home country in obedience to God's call, his wife went with him. She was sixty-five at the time. It took just as much faith in the Lord on her part to break family ties and pull up roots from the security of a place called "home." From that day on she made a home for her husband wherever he chose to pitch his tent. The broad expanse of Canaan became their home and they wandered from place to place in it.

Soon after they landed in this new country, a famine hit, and what did Abraham, that mighty man of faith, do? He ran. He fled to Egypt where there was food. But worse than that, he jeopardized his wife's welfare to save his own neck. Sarah was a stunning beauty, and Abraham was afraid he would be killed so that someone else could have her for his wife. So he compromisingly suggested, "Tell them you're my sister, not my wife, so they won't kill me." His total concern was for himself, his own skin, his own life. He was a coward and a cad at that moment.

We can only imagine the turmoil of Sarah's thoughts. This was her great big man for whom she had left everything to follow into unknown worlds. Now, when she needed him most, he let her down. He was her only physical tie with home. It was too far to pack her bags and run home to mother, or sister, or anyone. How did she get through? Peter gives the secret—she set her hope in God and submitted to her husband. The ultimate star in her life was not her husband, but God. She trusted God and did as her husband asked.

Anyone who sets his faith in another person, even the best person in the world, is bound to be disappointed. But if we set our hope in God, trust implicitly in him, we will never be disappointed. God didn't let Sarah down. He brought her through the confines of a heathen harem unscathed.

Sarah's story and example came up many times in the months that the Bible study was in progress. We reviewed it that morning with Wilma. We prayed together, and then she went home and spent the rest of the day in fasting and prayer. The Lord gave her peace even though she saw no immediate change in her husband. She doubled her efforts to be the best wife and mother possible and prayed for discipline not to let loose with cutting remarks. It wasn't easy. But in due course her husband gave up the struggle and turned his life over to Jesus Christ. Today he counts the Lord as an active partner in his business and he teaches a Sunday school class. If anyone would have suggested the latter chore to him a few months ago he would have laughed derisively.

The Bible doesn't waste words on principles which don't work. The greatest hindrance to their working is our unbelief. Sometimes, too, we may think we're submitting when we're not. This was true of Lillian. She became a Christian after attending several Bible study sessions. She was exuberantly happy. Next, the Lord delivered her from smoking. Her husband was so impressed with the change in her life that when her children balked at her attempt to have family devotions, he would call from the next room, "You kids, be quiet! Whatever has changed your mother is great, so shut up and listen to her."

The deliverance from smoking left her with an unsatisfied craving which she met with food. The pounds mounted rapidly and with it a strain in their marriage. Her husband didn't appreciate a fat wife. The strain upset Lillian and the more upset she became, the more she ate. She rationalized her weight in all kinds of ways, but the ultimate rationalization was, "Perhaps the Lord wants to teach my husband something by this."

I told her I didn't think it was her place to determine what God needed to teach her husband nor how he would do it. The point was that whether he was right or wrong, her husband didn't like her so overweight, and the only one who could do anything about it was herself.

When she stopped rationalizing, faced the issues squarely and accepted full responsibility for her condition, she put her trust in the Lord, submitted to the wishes of her husband, and went on a diet. Since that day she has lost sixty pounds, and she will be the first to say that it was accomplished on her knees.

An added bonus has been that her whole attitude toward her marriage has changed. She said recently, "I never realized how domineering I had been at home. It was *my* wishes that were most important. I got my way or else. Now I genuinely want to please my husband. Making him happy is more important than getting my way."

The Bible principle has worked in this home too. Lillian's husband and three of her children have followed her in personal faith in Jesus Christ.

In another situation after a woman came to know Christ, her husband didn't resist her commitment; he just remained totally indifferent to it. Then business caused a separation of the family for several months. Her husband became so lonely that he began to attend the church his wife had attended. It wasn't long before he too accepted

Christ. His comment at the time was, "I can't believe that I could have gone on for over forty years not knowing where I stood with God."

The family is again reunited and the wife's comment was, "I hope my husband will experience the same daily peace which I have had in my life."

Submission is the characteristic God expects of a wife whether her husband is an unbeliever, or intellectually beneath her, or with less spiritual interest or any other reason of incompatibility.

From our own experience in the Bible study group we know that husbands, no matter how stalwart their external defenses may be, are not impregnable to the Spirit of God. And very often the most effective weapon the Lord wields is a spiritually committed wife. Incidentally men who commit their lives to Christ don't sacrifice their masculinity. Christ makes them "whole" men.

For those who are still waiting for the Lord to work in the lives of their husbands, don't lose heart. Set your hope firmly in God, submit to your husband, speak with gentleness, and the Lord will take it from there.

# 12

## Women
## are People

The second year of the Bible study was started the first Wednesday after school opened. This year also found me as co-room mother with Meg for the 3rd and 4th grades. (My preschooler asked me one day, "Why are you a 'cold' room mother?")

Meg was an "alive" person. When she was around everything went into motion, usually in high gear! She was also "up tight" on life. In fact she was close to a nervous breakdown. Chain smoking and tranquilizers kept her going.

Meg had a Christian friend who had been praying for her for years. One of our Bible study members had repeatedly invited her to join us on Wednesday mornings. Then I came along as her co-room mother, and she felt trapped! As far as I can recall I invited her to the Bible study only once or twice. She gave me a number of excuses as to why she couldn't come, so the subject was dropped. Although nothing more was said, she felt impelled to tell me why she couldn't come almost every time she saw me. But she evidently ran out of "excuses," for one Wednesday morning she showed up!

The real surprise was when she came again the following week. She seemed to be in a fog. She was there, and yet she wasn't. I went to see her that afternoon. She told me of her fears, the greatest of which was a morbid fear of death. She felt physically ill and was sure she was going to die.

We read some scriptures together, and I asked her if she wouldn't like to invite Jesus Christ into her life. "No. I'm afraid," was her quick response. After praying I left her with a copy of Campus Crusades' *The Four Spiritual Laws.* My heart was heavy, and for a while Meg's attendance at the study became sporadic.

Then one morning she came to class when we were discussing the creation of man as recorded in Genesis. The discussion centered on the uniqueness of man, that he was created in the image of God, that he was created to have communion with God, that he had an eternal soul. Finally Meg queried, "Do you mean that man is created with a part of his being that is capable of seeking and knowing God?"

"Right," came the positive, emphatic answer.

"And," another woman quickly added, "man is never truly satisfied until he has found God."

What happened later that day is told by Meg, "I came home from Bible study that Wednesday feeling so bad I lay down. I felt backed up against a wall. Then and there in my room I cried out my need for Jesus Christ. I asked him for his help and his strength. I said, 'Take my life and run it because I'm doing a miserable job!' "

The Lord heard and answered Meg's cry. She became a new creation that day. Her spirit had found its rest in God. A year and a half has passed since then. One of the most obvious changes in Meg is her aura of serenity, which has been accomplished without the help of cigarettes or tranquilizers. She needs neither. Let me hasten to add that this does not imply a judgment on people dependent on smoking or tranquilizers, or—does it?

Meg is now a Bible study leader and also very active at school. She was in charge of a recent fund-raising luncheon sponsored by the PTA. She worked hard, organized it well, but all the frantic nervous atmosphere which would have been characteristic before were gone this time. She said, "I just turned the whole affair over to the Lord and let him run it." It was a huge success. Compliments poured in on what a good job Meg had done, and frank amazement was felt at her calmness through all of it. Meg isn't ashamed to tell anyone that the credit belongs to the Lord and not to her.

Seeing God at work in the lives of individuals is always exciting. Jesus Christ never destroys a personality. He enhances it. He also has a useful purpose for every individual life. We're not part of a mass production line created in exactly the same way to do exactly the same thing as the next person. This aspect of individual value and acceptance of individual roles in life had great appeal for the women who felt they weren't anything special and had nothing to offer anyone else. Some felt bound by their past.

One woman resented the fact that she hadn't had the same education opportunities that others had enjoyed. Another woman had been tossed from one home to another as a child, experiencing very little love in the process. Another woman grew up in a home where she was made to feel she was a total liability, of no good to anyone. Another woman said, "I grew up in a home where adultery was the order of the day. My mother had a succession of men spending the night. It's not easy to throw off those early impressions and chart a totally different course for myself." To all of these women the knowledge that God loved them and valued them as individuals was a tremendous revelation.

A great deal of modern psychiatry has emphasized the past background of individuals to give a reason for the way they feel and act in the present. It's true that we are the sum total of our lives up to this point. The past is important in shaping our values and goals. We cannot ignore it. However, it is interesting to notice in the Bible that God does not especially favor those who have come from backgrounds abundant with love and possessions and education, nor does he expect less of those who have come from poor, harsh or deprived backgrounds. In other words, he leaves no room for pride on the one hand or groveling self-pity on the other. Yet, we see a lot of both today.

There are many people born into a certain circumstance or station in life who feel they are a little better than the next person. There are others who would rather bask in the sympathy of a neglected childhood and excuse present failures "because my mother didn't love me" than to face squarely their individual responsibility and do something about it.

One woman had been going to a psychiatrist for over a year and he had delved into every recess of her past to find a reason for her current depression. She said, "I finally realized that I was an adult totally responsible for the way I acted and thought regardless of my past." And she stopped going to the psychiatrist.

Three of the early leaders of the nation of Israel came from a poor, deprived slave home. They weren't free; they were slaves. Two of them had none of the economic advantages we value so highly today. They were cruelly treated by their masters. One son got an education and had material possessions at his disposal, but he was raised in a school system that rejected the God in which his family believed. Yet out of this chaotic background came Moses, Aaron and Miriam, dynamic leaders of their nation. They overcame all the disadvantages of their early environment. How? By faith.

They accepted each day as coming from the hand of God and trusted him in it. They didn't allow bitterness for past deprivation destroy the Lord's plan for them.

If we nurture resentment and bitterness for past wrongs done to us we will effectively kill our usefulness to the Lord. One of the women who has been in the Bible study refuses to forgive her daughter for a wrong she has done against her. She openly admits her bitterness against her daughter and won't allow the Lord to remove it. She thinks about it, feeds it, and it keeps growing. She doesn't want to come to the study because "I'm not walking with God." And she won't walk in fellowship with the Lord until she lets him uproot her resentment. The Bible calls bitterness "a root" that, if allowed to grow, will cause trouble and poison others as well.

One woman said to me, "I may forgive a person

for what she has done, but I'll sure never forget it." Well, that's not really forgiveness at all. When God forgives, he also forgets. We're to do the same.

Another woman I know has harbored resentment for over thirty years for ill-treatment received from others. She's unhappy and she spreads her unhappiness everywhere she goes.

A Catholic nun who lives and works in a Chicago ghetto which was gutted by fiery riots following Martin Luther King's assassination made this pertinent observation afterward: "The secret to survival in hard and even unjust circumstances is lack of bitterness. Bitterness is self-destructive, such as we have seen in the riots in the ghetto. When we allow bitterness to dominate our lives, we destroy ourselves."

Christ enables us to rise above the past. The Apostle Paul exhorts, "Forgetting what lies behind . . . press on!"[1] There's too much to do to allow outselves to get hung up on what might have been. Now is the hour. God can take you right where you are and make you into a useful person for his purposes, complete and fulfilled—if you will let him.

This matter of acknowledging resentment, accepting full personal responsibility for my actions before God, admitting, "I have failed and I can

[1]Phil. 3:13-14 (RSV).

blame no one but myself," came close to home to every woman in the class. Having reached this point of admission, it was comforting to have the Lord come in to forgive and cleanse and make new. It helped with the problem of guilt too.

A college coed who was a new Christian asked me recently, "Is there any hope for me to have a wholesome fulfilled marriage someday? I've already gone the whole route in sex. I know God has forgiven me, but I feel so guilty." Guilt for past sins plagues a lot of people. Not even time will remove it.

The Old Testament tells the story of Joseph whose brothers out of jealousy sold him into slavery in Egypt. They lied about what had happened to their father. The lie stood for twenty years. But then hard times hit the family and in their distress the brothers said, "We are *guilty* concerning our brother . . . therefore is this distress come upon us."[2] Twenty years with no one else knowing what had actually happened still hadn't removed the guilt from their consciences.

Twenty years of "covering up" had landed one woman in a psychiatric ward. She sat in the cabin where we were vacationing and told my husband and me the story. She has been a common-law wife for all those years. Her "husband" had never felt it was important enough to legalize their

[2]Gen. 42:22 (RSV).

marriage. He provided for her and their children, and she was faithful to him. But there was always that gnawing insecurity. She felt she had to work twice as hard to "keep" him so that he wouldn't leave her for someone else. The strain and tension built up until he had her committed to a psychiatric hospital.

In the hospital she picked up a Gideon Bible, began to read it and then called for a nurse.

"Who are the Gideons?" she asked.

"They are an organization of people who distribute Bibles," the nurse replied.

"Can I talk to one?"

"I'll see."

The nurse was able to contact a man associated with the Gideons in that area. He and his wife befriended this woman, visited with her, answered her questions, until one day she reached the point of deciding to trust Christ.

She went home from the hospital and talked her "husband" into getting married. "I don't know how I got him to agree," she said. "I guess the Lord did it." It was such a relief to her not to have to live a lie anymore.

The Bible solution for guilt is confession. "If we confess our sins to God, we can trust him, for he does what is right—he will forgive us our sins and make us clean from all our wrongdoing."[3]

[3] I John 1:9 (*Good News for Modern Man*).

**God forgives and cleanses when we confess.**
Then we have to forgive ourselves, and this is often
the hardest thing to do. We keep feeling guilty
even when the sin has been confessed and forgiven
by God. The Lord said to Peter, "Do not consider
anything unclean that God has declared clean."[4] If
we have been cleansed by God we are actually
calling God a liar in calling ourselves unclean!

Christ's redemption is great enough to allow a
young woman to experience God's best in marriage
even though she has lost her virginity. His redemption can also remove the guilt of a hasty marriage
necessitated by pregnancy and transform that marriage into one of strength and honor to him.

As one woman expressed it after relating a
rather sordid past, "The Bible study helped me to
accept what I was and then I was able to ask the
Lord to forgive me and still love me."

There is no liberty quite as great as the liberty
of a clear conscience. Thank God that's what the
gospel is all about. It's the good news which tells
us how to cut through the chains of bondage to
ourselves, bondage to the past, bondage to guilt. It
was marvelous to watch the Lord liberate the
women in the Bible in these very areas. It bore out
the truth of Christ's statement "If the Son makes
you free, you will be free indeed."[5]

[4] John 8:36 (*Good News for Modern Man*).
[5] John 8:36 (RSV).

# 13

**Love
is a
Risk**

"I lie awake nights sometimes, thinking about her.
I wonder, in her devotion to an ideal, is she taking
unnecessary risks?"

The question arose over Jesus' statement "If
any man would come after me, let him deny
himself, and take up his cross and follow me."[1]

What was the cost of discipleship? In thinking
about a reply, one of the women told of a young
woman from her church who had decided to teach
in a slum school in a "bad" part of the city. Her
parents and friends considered it unsafe. She
admired the girl for her unselfish zeal and desire to
give herself to those who needed her talents most,
but where do you draw the line between courage

[1] Mark 8:34 (RSV).

and recklessly throwing caution to the winds?

"She really had everybody in the church business meeting squirming when she talked about what she intended to do," she added. "All of us felt rather selfish and unsacrificial when she got through. But how do you know how involved to get? Is she wrong? Are we wrong? What's the answer? How big a price does God expect of us?"

"How big was the price for Christ?" someone else asked. "What did 'the cross' mean to him?"

"It meant giving his life," was the quick reply.

"Does that mean we are expected to take all kinds of risks and be willing to die to be true followers of Christ?"

"Maybe the answer lies in motivation," another woman suggested. "If this young woman is doing what she's doing because she's following an idealistic dream she may be headed for trouble."

"Disillusionment will hit a bit harder when her 'dream' doesn't measure up to her expectations," contributed someone else. "However, if she goes because she feels sincerely that this is what God wants her to do, she has a firmer base for the risks involved. This doesn't mean that no harm could come to her. Hundreds of people have suffered and even died because they followed Jesus Christ. But at least she's not out there hanging onto a limb by herself, and she has someone to go to when disillusionment strikes."

"This is all well and good. Obedience—motivation and all that. But how does this apply to us right here? We're all homemakers. None of us is going to march off to a slum. We can't. We have families right here expecting us to cook their supper tonight. How does the cost of discipleship apply to me?"

"I know one area where there's a big price tag—my attitude toward the racial problem."

"Oh boy, now you've hit pay dirt! You should have heard the women in the beauty shop! They were all discussing the Negro family that has moved into the area. Everybody is worried about property values. A lot of people are talking of selling and moving farther out."

"It's a lot more than talk! Have you seen all the for-sale signs popping up?"

"Some people say they're moving because of the high school. They're afraid of the riots they've had."

"Ah—now we're getting to some of the 'risks' involved!"

"Yes, but do you really think it's right to risk your children's welfare? I can see taking risks yourself, but your kids? That's something else again."

"I guess that brings us right back to motivation. Why am I living where I am living?"

"Because it's the only place we could find a decent house we could afford!"

"Nothing wrong with that reason. But supposing the area keeps changing. Would you move? And, if so, why?"

"I don't know that I can answer that honestly. My feelings are mixed on the issue. But I'm still hung up on the matter of the safety of my children."

"Is God big enough to take care of us and our children, or isn't he?"

"Yes, I believe he is. But can we expect his protection if we take unnecessary risks?"

"Back to motivation. If I am where I am because God has put me there, then I can have all the confidence in the world that he will look out for my welfare and for the welfare of my children. However, if I didn't settle here with any conviction that it was what God wanted, I would still have to check my motivations for making a move. Do we ever solve problems by running from them?"

"I guess not. If we can't prove God's power in the place where we are right now, we'll never prove his power anywhere else either. The place of greatest 'safety' is in the will of God."

"I can certainly appreciate that particular point. Because my parents were missionaries I was sent to a boarding school for my education. This boarding school became a prisoner-of-war camp during World War II. It was hardly a 'safety zone' for kids. Yet, we couldn't have run to a safer place if we had wanted to. My parents were in the position they were in because they had obeyed the leadings of God. They were motivated by love and devotion to Jesus Christ. And they dared to believe that the Lord who had brought them there could bring them and their daughter through this dangerous situation. The Lord didn't let them down."

"Somehow we expect missionaries to trust the Lord for the difficult situations, but here at home we don't involve the Lord. We find our own way out."

"Isn't it interesting? Our churches spent millions to send missionaries across the seas, but let a mission field move next door, and we run for the hills! And often we spend even more doing it."

"I find it very sad. Why are Christians so afraid?"

"Who knows? I guess we have let our God shrink. We don't really believe he's able to change other people's lives, especially if those people are covered with black skin."

"What scares me is the rise in hatred of people for each other. You can feel it in the PTA meetings when bussing or integration is discussed. You can feel it at church. If Christians are motivated by love, there's precious little of it floating around."

"I wonder if they think that heaven will be segregated?"

"The Bible certainly doesn't give that picture. I

love the description in Revelation where it says of Christ, "Thou wast slain and by thy blood didst ransom men for God from every tribe and tongue and people and nation, and hast made them *a* kingdom and priests to our God.'[2] It's *one* kingdom, and all are there on the same basis. Everyone has been redeemed by the blood of Jesus Christ."

"If we sincerely believed that was true, how can any Christian be a follower of Jesus Christ and say of a person with different color or language, 'I'll be glad to live with you in heaven, but don't expect it of me on earth!'?"

How indeed?

The "racial" question has torn our country apart from coast to coast. Our community was not exempt. In the Bible study the women for the most part showed a genuine concern for doing the right thing. A few clung tenaciously to build-in prejudices.

One woman said, "I know I'm prejudiced, and I don't mind saying so!" However, even she was willing to be changed. She phoned me one day after she had started to work in a certain place, and laughingly declared, "I guess the Lord is really working on my prejudice. You know, I'm the only white woman working in this shop, and I'm learning to actually love the women I work with!"

[2] Rev. 5:9-10 (RSV).

Most of us feel though that the whole problem is just too big to cope with. The question keeps coming up, What can *I* do that will mean anything? I don't feel right about participating in marches or demonstrating, so what's left?

How about loving the person next door? Cultivate the friendship of someone who is of a different color and cultural background. Don't be intimidated by "panic" pushers. Sort out your motivations honestly before the Lord and pray for his love to flow through you. Be prepared for the "freeze" treatment by others who don't share your convictions. One woman in the Bible study made a point of welcoming new neighbors in the community. They were black. Her children made friends with the new children. But the woman who extended the friendship was treated with a lot of "cold shoulders" by her neighbors, and her children were called "nigger lovers." Actually, they were lovers of God who were willing to be motivated by his love to touch all people, to be "color-blind."

After all Christ doesn't see skins. It's man "that looks on the outward appearance"; God looks at the heart. And all hearts are black unless they have been cleansed by the blood of Christ.

"What if I extend my love and friendship, as we have discussed it, and it's rejected by the person or people to whom I extend it?" was a recent question raised in the Bible study.

"That would be a real test of discipleship wouldn't it?"

Whether people respond or reject doesn't change the fact that Christ expects his followers to love.

It was Ethel, a friend, a neighbor, a member of the Bible study who happened to be black, who asked one morning, "What is love?"

We turned to I Corinthians 13 for the answer—"Love is patient and kind; love is not jealous, or conceited, or proud; love is not ill-mannered, or selfish, or irritable; love does not keep a record of wrongs; love is not happy with evil, but is happy with the truth. Love never gives up: its faith, hope, and patience never fail. Love is eternal."[3]

Jesus said to his disciples, "A new commandment I give to you, that you love one another; even as I have loved you, that you also love one another. By this all men will know that you are my disciples, if you have love for one another."[4]

[3]I Cor. 13:4-8 (*Good News for Modern Man*).
[4]John 13:34-35 (RSV).

# 14

## To Grow
## is to
## Change

Rita and I were on the way to Bible study one morning and stopped to buy coffee rolls. It was Rita's turn to bring them. After her purchase she got into the car, looked at the price slip and said, "Hey, that lady in the bakery only charged me for one dozen rolls, but I bought two dozen! Guess I'll have to go back and pay for the other dozen."

When she took in the additional money, the lady acted as though Rita had holes in her head. Why would anyone come back voluntarily with money? After all, if you got away with it, it's your "good luck," and it's just too bad the other person was so stupid.

But Rita's action represented the change of attitude and change in values that many of the women experienced in the Bible study. For most of the women there weren't big dramatic changes, but small meaningful ones in their daily lives.

The fact that they attended a Bible study regularly was a shock in itself to neighbors, family and friends. But all these people learned to accept it as a part of life. As my Avon representative put it one day, "I knew you wouldn't be home Wednesday morning!" Nena's phone even stopped ringing on Wednesday mornings.

I remember one spring afternoon calling on a lady whose son and his friend were filling in applications to be able to take advantage of a suburban swimming pool. They were falsifying their addresses so that they wouldn't have to pay the "outsider" fees charged those who didn't live in the community of the pool.

As I walked up, her son asked, "Mom, how old am I supposed to be?"

"You own age, of course!" she retorted with obvious embarassment that I had walked in right then.

This is something which this woman wouldn't do today because her sense of values has been changed by Jesus Christ. Because you "get away with it" makes you neither smart nor right.

Another woman said she had found her "fuse" had gotten longer. She didn't blow up quite as fast as she used to; her reactions were changing.

There's a term being thrown around a lot these days. It's called "overreaction." What it actually means seems a little uncertain. How it differs from just plain "reaction" is unclear.

Our reactions reveal what is inside. In other words, if you tip over a jug of milk, milk is going to spill all over the floor. What comes out is what is already inside. And, if it's your child that spills the milk on a freshly waxed floor, what's going to spill out of you at him? What is already inside!

The Bible says, "Out of the abundance of the heart the mouth speaks."[1] Yet how often we'll say, "Well, under the circumstances, how would you expect me to react?"

Or we may rationalize the anger with "I was tired," or "This isn't my day," or "This has been a hard week," etc. The fact remains that what comes out is what is already inside. The crisis doesn't produce the reaction; it merely reveals it. So, "overreaction" must mean that we're tipped over a little farther and the dregs at the bottom pour out.

A recent comment by one of the women was, "I hadn't realized how much change the Lord worked in my life until the other day when one of my children knocked over a gallon of ceiling paint on a brand new floor, and I was amazed at my reaction. I stayed calm and cool and treated it as an accident, which it was. It wasn't too long ago that a crisis like that would have sent me, and everyone else, into orbit!"

[1]Matt. 12:34 (RSV).

Now, of course, none of the women in the study would claim that she *never* loses her "cool." But the pattern has changed and the "fuse" has lengthened as Christ has taken over greater control.

The women developed a love for each other and a sincere concern for one another's problems. There was that sense of friendship, and warmth and "belonging" which all of us need.

We have learned and are still learning how to face life realistically, to accept our personal roles without envy or jealousy of someone else's lot in life, to live without fear of death or illness or tragedy. We have learned that we don't need to build a protective cocoon around ourselves, as does one woman I know of, who refuses to read sad stories, watch sad TV programs, think glum thoughts, go to funerals, or visit sick people in the hospital. Living as though death and sadness don't exist doesn't change their reality. They do exist. And it's far more realistic to face each day as it comes, with joy or sadness, with Christ at your side. He gives a security and joy that no protective cocoon we might build around ourselves could ever match.

The women learned to give of themselves, of what they had for someone else. One of the women who gave the most never attended a single Bible study session. She was our baby-sitter, Vicki.

A good baby-sitter is a vital factor in a

well-functioning Bible study. She should be the subject of prayer when starting one. Women need to feel that their children are being well cared for while they are involved in their study time. They can concentrate better on the subject at hand if they aren't worrying about their children at the same time. For this reason, it is usually better to have the children in a separate home than the one the study is in. The cries of children in the same house can be very distracting, when every mother jumps up, just sure that that is *her* child who is crying.

Our first baby-sitter was a lovely Christian woman who took excellent care of the children, and the children loved her. Surgery necessitated her stopping, but she found us a grand replacement.

Vicki has been the steady sitter for three years. She could probably write a book on all the families as seen through the eyes of their children! (We hope she won't!)

Vicki viewed her baby-sitting as her ministry for the Lord. She loved the children committed to her care. She said it was very helpful for her to discover that her children were normal! They weren't the naughtiest ones around after all. She learned patience—she had to! Some days we left as many as seventeen preschoolers at her doorstep.

At first we paid her in proportion to the number of children she had. Some study groups set a flat rate in which all the women share. When there are more women out, the less cost it is to each mother. All agree though, that it's worth every penny to study in peace and quiet.

Then Vicki decided one day that she didn't want to be paid anymore. She felt that as long as she was paid her motives were selfish, and she couldn't really call it a "ministry" to the Lord. Her contribution to the class could never be measured. We thank God for her.

One of the nice things about giving "as unto the Lord" is that we will never suffer loss. He returns a hundredfold what paltry little we may give to him. The returns may not come from those who received the gift, but the returns will be there. It's impossible to "outgive" God.

The Bible says we should be "servants of Christ, doing the will of God from the heart, rendering service with a good will as to the Lord and not to men, knowing *that whatever good any one does, he will receive the same again from the Lord.*"[2]

Somehow I can hear the Lord saying very specifically someday, "Inasmuch as ye have done it unto one of the least of these . . . ye have done it unto me."[3]

Another evidence of a changed value was voiced by one of the women when she said, "For the first

[2] Eph. 6:6-8 (RSV).
[3] Matt. 25:40.

time in my life something like getting a new couch just isn't that important to me! Most of my friends and relatives are financially secure and have lovely homes filled with the latest of everything. Knowing it was wrong to covet didn't make me not do it! Every time I visited one of their homes I would come home and cry. I tried to tell myself I was giving up things for the sake of the Lord, but in my heart I knew I was just plain jealous.

"Since I'm spending time in the Bible, I'm reminded daily of my spiritual inheritance in Christ. One of my greatest joys now is in making contacts with my neighbors and friends and praying for their needs. I'm content with my furniture and I can genuinely enjoy the luxury of my friends' homes without envy. Praise the Lord for that victory!"

Yet another interesting effect of the Bible study was in church relationships. One woman declared quite frankly, "I don't attend church as often as I used to. If I want to know about current events or books, I'd rather do my reading for myself. When I go to church I want to hear about the Bible and God."

Many women moved from local churches which only fulfilled the function of "social clubs" in their lives, to churches where the emphasis was on the Bible and its practical effect on daily living. Four families now attend my local church.

Other women consider their churches a

"mission field" and take an active part in teaching the Bible in their Sunday school classes.

We didn't advise anyone to change churches. But changes came as women became dissatisfied with any pulpit which did not clearly preach from the Bible. And some who were already attending Bible-centered churches found a new appreciation for the truth that was being taught there.

In dozens of ways women in the study spoke of how their homes, attitudes, values, goals had been changed. Christ worked the change. The Bible study was merely the vehicle for producing the change.

# 15

**Hot Line
to
God?**

One of the many stories told of George Mueller, who ran an orphanage for hundreds of children by prayer and faith, pertained to the purchase of some property. The orphanage needed to be enlarged and, on hearing that some suitable property was for sale, he went to see the owner.

Mr. Mueller made an offer for the property, and the seller laughed in his face.

"Why", he said, "that property is worth far more than that. I couldn't possibly let it go for such a ridiculous price."

"Well, that's my offer, sir," replied Mr. Mueller. "Please consider it." And he left.

A few days later the owner laughingly recounted the episode to a friend. His friend also knew

Mr. Mueller and said, quite seriously, "You had better give it to him at the price he offered or he'll pray to his God until you give it to him for nothing!"

Many references to prayer have been made in this story, and its importance could never be overestimated. We didn't really have a "hot line" or special "in" with God any more than anyone else. But God did work as we prayed.

The prayer session before each Bible study became as vital as the study itself. We prayed for ourselves, our children, our husbands. We prayed for our schools, our communities, the leaders of our nation.

We prayed for sons in Vietnam. One mother said, "When our son was in Vietnam God answered prayer and watched over him. Three different times he was close to not coming home, but by the grace of God—when a jeep turned over on him, he came out with just a broken leg—when the ammo truck he was driving went into a skid on a muddy road and ended up hanging over a cliff, it stayed there until he was freed—and when he was in a convoy of trucks, two trucks in front of his hit land mines."

This was miraculous preservation. But we prayed for Vicki's brother too, and his plane went down in the Gulf of Tonkin and he was never found.

Is God unfair in the way he answers? No. We

don't know why he answers in one way or the other, but we can always trust in his character which is good, absolutely just, and full of love. He doesn't make mistakes. He isn't arbitrary. He doesn't show favoritism.

I suppose the biggest effect in the Bible study was the growing consciousness by the women that the Lord wasn't removed from them in unreachable realms. He was present. He cared. He listened. He worked.

One woman put it this way: "Opening prayer for guidance, and special requests are a very vital part of our meeting. It has given me the feeling of sitting with our Lord and speaking directly to him about our life here on earth. We may have had as many as twenty-five persons in the room at the time, but I think we each had the feeling of being alone with God."

One of Nena's neighbors who had been invited to the study but never came, had a stroke one night. Her husband called Nena and Bob over. The doctor gave her a fifty-fifty chance for recovery.

Nena asked the women to pray, and they did. The neighbor recovered, and when she came home, Nena invited her again to the study. She hesitated until Nena said, "At least come and meet these ladies who have prayed for you." She came—and stayed. She became one of the class regulars.

We have seen enough response to prayer that one woman burst out one day, "Please *don't* pray about that problem. I'm not up to receiving any answers yet!"

Prayer was our life line.

Anytime God is at work building, you can rest assured that Satan will be working just as hard trying to tear down.

One of the women said, "I think the devil does more work on Wednesday and Sunday mornings than at any other time of the week. Just when I want to get to Bible study or church the car won't start, we can't find Billy's other shoe, Tommy doesn't have an ironed shirt to wear, the phone rings, the furnace goes on the blink, or something."

The problems may be minor irritations, personality conflicts, or major crises.

One major crisis was the suicide of one of the women's brother-in-law. It meant shifting gears for leading, taking care of the children in the family while the mother and father flew to the funeral. The suicide victim was in his thirties, a father of three, a Ph.D. candidate. It was a tragedy, and all of us suffered together. When our Bible study member returned she said, "We really felt held up by your prayers."

Personality conflicts, people with touchy feelings, can be pressing problems. We had occasional blowups when women got on each other's nerves. There's no substitute for saying, "I'm sorry" if you lose your temper. For some people an apology is so hard they almost gag on it. Touchy Christians are often some of Satan's most effective tools. Prayer is the best remedy for someone who really bugs you. Pray for that person, and don't start off by saying, "Lord, help her to be nicer." Start by thanking God for some good quality in her. If you have to stay on your knees a half hour to think of something, stay there until you can honestly thank God for that person you can't stand! It's very hard to dislike someone for whom you pray in sincerity. She may not change, but your attitude toward her will change. It's worth trying.

The weather often seemed to work against us. The Bible study continued in spite of the blizzard of 1967 with its six-foot snowdrifts. That same year our closing dinner in the summer went on despite a torrential deluge which closed roads and filled viaducts with water. We waded through water a foot deep to reach the restaurant where the dinner was held. These things make the occasions more memorable and produce hardier souls!

One Bible study leader asked recently, "What on earth are we doing wrong? Everything has been happening to us!" Their group was experiencing some major conflicts, including the nervous breakdown of one member.

I replied, "It's not what you're doing wrong, it's what you're doing right that has the devil all shaken up."

Two women had recently become Christians in that group. Satan never likes people who tamper with his territory. If there is conflict we should be glad! It's evidence that God is at work. There's far more to fear when things go smoothly all the time.

Paul encouraged the Christians at Ephesus to "put on the whole armor of God, that you may be able to stand against the wiles of the devil. For we are not contending against flesh and blood, but against the wiles of the devil. For we are not contending against flesh and blood, but against the principalities, against the powers, against the world rulers of this present darkness, against the spiritual hosts of wickedness in the heavenly places."[1]

This enemy can be frightening, but the Lord gives us all the weapons we need to stand. And one of those weapons is prayer.

One recent breakthrough in our prayer time is having women who have never prayed out loud in their lives before, taking part in the prayer sessions. Some of our new leaders used to protest, "I just can't pray out loud. I freeze up. I don't think I'll ever do it."

We encourage them to pray aloud at home just to get used to the sound of their own voices; then when they do pray, just to say one sentence.

Meg came for quite a while before she worked up the courage to pray in the group. But one day

[1] Eph. 6:11-12 (RSV).

she did, and she hasn't stopped since! In fact, she was even asked to give the invocation at a PTA meeting one evening.

We sometimes pass around prayer requests on slips of paper and ask everyone in the group to take one, and pray for it. They don't have to begin with a "Dear Lord" or end with "Amen," they just talk to God. Rosalind Rinker's book *Prayer— Conversing with God*[2] has many helpful thoughts along this line.

After a recent prayer session before a class, one of our ladies looked up and said, "I think that's the first time I've prayed out loud in 23 years!"

They all found that after they had done it once, it was a lot easier the next time.

Learning to have a daily personal "quiet time" was another milestone. We spent one whole morning going through the little booklet *Manna in the Morning*[3] by Stephen Olford, and gave each woman a copy.

The following week we asked them to share what they had received from the Lord that week. It was absolutely thrilling to see all the notebooks open up as they shared ideas and concepts which they had gotten from the Bible all on their own. It's pretty hard to beat the Holy Spirit as a teacher.

[2](Grand Rapids: Zondervan, 1959).
[3](Chicago: Moody, 1965).

Quiet times are firm habits in many homes now. They don't have to take long hours of a mother's busy day. One woman said that when she had a set time in the morning it helped to gear her thoughts the rest of the day. She was more likely to pray while ironing if she had taken the time to be on her knees in the morning.

Another woman says she often finds herself in earnest prayer even while brushing her teeth!

Over and over again the thoughts the Lord has given me in the morning from the Bible are the very thoughts needed by someone else who may phone or drop in.

It is not without reason that the Lord lists the Scriptures and prayer as effective weapons of spiritual warfare.

He tells us to "take . . . the sword of the Spirit, which is the word of God. Pray at all times in the Spirit, with all prayer and supplication. To that end keep alert with all perseverance."[4]

"For the weapons of our warfare are not worldly but have divine power to destroy strongholds."[5]

[4] Eph. 6:17 (RSV).
[5] II Cor. 10:4 (RSV).

# 16

**The Name
of the Game
Is Commitment**

On a recent chilly December day, twenty-five of
our women met together to have lunch. In spite of
the cold outside, warm happy fellowship prevailed
inside.

Looking around at the group of women made
me think of King David's experience in the Old
Testament. Before he became king, David hid in a
cave to escape King Saul's frequent attempts on
his life. His family joined him in his hideout as did
"every one who was in distress, and every one who
was in debt, and every one who was discon-
tented."[1] If they were in trouble, it was David
they went to.

[1] I Sam. 22:2 (RSV).

It was a motley crew of people who looked for shelter in that cave. The one thing they had in common was David himself, "and he became captain over them." These very same men, under David's leadership, are later referred to as "David's mighty men."

Jesus Christ was the one who had gathered around him our group of women from all sorts of backgrounds with a variety of problems and needs. Under his leadership the Alices, Janes, Jills and others were becoming mighty women of God whose impact was being felt in their homes and communities, and whose potential for further influence in these areas was tremendous. We could sense it just in the table conversation at the lunch that day.

One of the women, expecting her fifth child, had summed it up earlier like this: "When we have committed our lives to Christ we can no longer sit back as spectators. We must be willing to put our faith and beliefs into action. We should study and feed on the Word of God every day—letting the works of Christ be evident in us. We must not try to walk alone ever again, for we now know that the living Christ in us will guide us and show us the way every day of the year."

Edith was at the lunch. Her invalid mother had died recently. Right up to the end she went every day to the nursing home to help care for her mother, and she was happy to do so. Many other elderly people in the home, whose own families neglected them, thought Edith belonged to them as well. Her cheerfulness and love spread out to all.

She could so easily have said, "My mother doesn't even know me now, so why bother going day after day?" But her Christianity wouldn't let her write off her filial responsibility so easily. She hasn't lost those last four years of her life. People who serve Christ are never losers.

Rhoda was at the luncheon, looking as healthy as ever.

Maria was there too. She had once made the comment, "A Christian living in today's world has a greater need than ever of Christ. Evil surrounds him and could overwhelm him, but if he has Christ he'll overcome the world."

Maria is both a sweet Christian and a devout Catholic who is putting into practice her strong desire to start a Bible study in Spanish. She is fluent in the language and would like to share Christ's love with others in her community who have no one else to talk to them about the Bible in words they understand.

And across the table from me sat Jean, who asked, "Remember our first Bible study, Winnie?"

"Sure do. How could I forget?"

Jean had been there. She had also been a rather sporadic participant for the next three years, full of questions, yet visibly resistant to the answers. At the lunch, though, I sensed she was talking like a different person, so I asked her later if she had changed her thinking.

She replied simply, "Yes, I've made a commitment of my life to Christ. The Bible study has been the most meaningful thing in my life. I learned there that to be a Christian you don't have to know all the answers first before you decide. It's a matter of taking Christ by faith. Now I'm learning as I go along."

I was listening eagerly, thankfully. She went on. "I've also learned there's a great big difference between being a "good" person and being a Christian. Though I've always been a 'good' person, I still wasn't a Christian. Yet nobody could have forced me into my decision. I had to arrive there myself.

"Now the Bible study is an established part of my life. It's greatest effect in our home is when the children bring up questions and I can say to them, 'I know where we can get the answer for that,' and we open our Bibles."

One of the most familiar faces—Nena's—was missing at the luncheon. In her place were many new women meeting each other for the first time. For the group gathered that day represented not just one Bible study group, but four.

Due to the location of her husband's business, Nena and her family had moved. The Lord used the move to divide the Bible study into four smaller study groups. Three of these groups are being led by women who either accepted Christ or came into a position of firmer commitment to him through the first Bible study. Four other ladies who left the original group have also started brand-new studies of their own in their communities. Even in the Philippines a little group has formed around one of our former study members who, with her husband, serves there as a missionary. To date, eight or nine have sprung from our original group. The outreach is multiplying by division.

Neighborhood Bible studies are not the final word in evangelism. But they are one means of communicating Jesus Christ which God seems to be blessing in a singular way.

Bible studies don't save people, Christ does. The point is that God is at work all around us. We can get in on the action if we make ourselves available to him and are willing to "open our mouths." The Lord isn't dependent on any one individual to do his work, but he usually chooses to work through those individuals who depend wholly on him. Someone has said, "There is no limit to what God can do through you, if you don't care who gets the credit."

And the late Dr. Martin Luther King is quoted as saying, "All I want to leave behind is a committed life." No one can deny that he died totally committed to a cause in which he deeply believed. He had a dream and an ideal which he doggedly pursued and which cost him his life.

A missionary who fled China when the Communists gained control, told of one town held by the Communists in an area where the nationalist forces at that point were stronger. As the nationalist army advanced it seemed certain the town would easily succumb to their superior strength.

On seeing this, the missionary asked the Communist officer, "Since defeat seems certain in this situation, why don't you surrender?"

The officer replied, "I would gladly lay down my life to advance Communism one mile."

He was committed to an ideal. His life was a small price for him to pay for what he believed.

Christ has so much more to offer. Then why aren't his followers more committed to him? Should he receive so much less devotion from us?

The Apostle Paul challenges us individually like this: "And he [Christ] died for all, that those who live might live no longer for themselves but for him who for their sake died and was raised."[2]

Neighborhood Bible studies are a vehicle in which a homemaker can express her commitment to Christ and be used by him without being removed from her essential place as wife and mother. One of the most poignant comments as to whether time so spent is really worth it or not came from Nena's ten-year-old son as they were

[2] II Cor. 5:15 (RSV).

rushing to get the house ready for the study one morning. When Nena complained of how little time there was to get everything done, her son retorted, "But, Mom, if you hadn't had the Bible study, we might never have got to know God."